# owning a

## the official guide

The Stationery Off

Published by The Stationery Office for the Department of the Environment, Transport and the Regions (DETR) under licence from the Controller of Her Majesty's Stationery Office.


The information in this book provides guidance and should not be read as a substitute for the law. Information, including prices, are correct at time of going to press. New editions are published periodically. You can check the details of new editions www.ukstate.com

Commercial websites suggested in this book are for information purposes only. DETR does not endorse or recommend any product or service identified above any other and has not reviewed them for their content. DETR excludes any warranty, express or implied, as to the quality or completeness of the content of these websites. Views expressed by third parties are their own. This information has not been tailored for your particular requirements. DETR does not make any representation or warranty of any kind as to the operation of the websites. Your use of the Web will be on the basis of cash sites' own terms and conditions which you should read in each case. DETR is not liable to you or any third party for any errors or delays in the content of the websites or for any action taken in reliance on it. So far as is allowed by law DETR will not be liable for any direct, indirect or consequential loss arising from the use of these websites or from your access of other material on the Internet via Web links from these sites.

ISBN 011 552214 X

A CIP catalogue record for this book is available from the British Library.

# Introduction

Buying a car may be the largest sum of money you will ever spend on a single item. This book gives information on what to look for when buying a car, what events you have to deal with once you own it and the steps to take when selling it on.

This innovative book has its own website which gives access to further official information and together they provide all you need to know about owning a car.

Official information is already available from various sources, but it is not often clear which Department or Agency to contact, so we have brought all this information into one place for easy access. It's information you can rely on because it is written by the experts who are familiar with all the legislation.

The website acts as a portal by enabling you to get straight to the information required without having to search through each government website individually.

As well as being a useful gift for the new driver, *Owning a Car* is also an essential reference book for every household.

William Rickett

Willie Rickett
Director of Transport Strategy and Planning
Chairman DVO Strategy Board

## Contents





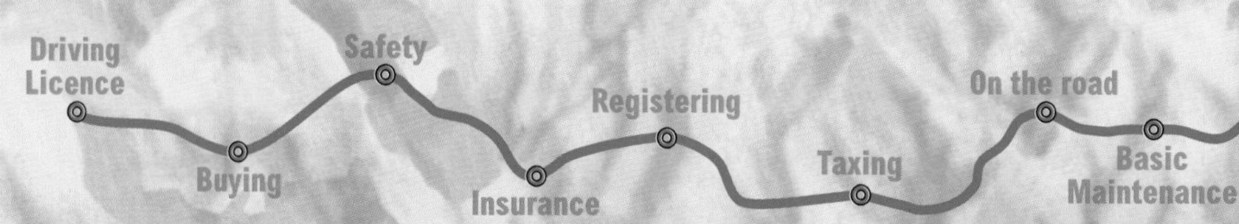

Driving Licence
Buying
Safety
Insurance
Registering
Taxing
On the road
Basic Maintenance

MOT Test
Breakdowns
Going Green
Security
Going Abroad
Selling
Further Information

Driving Licence
Buying
Safety
Insurance
Registering
Taxing
On the road
Basic Maintenance

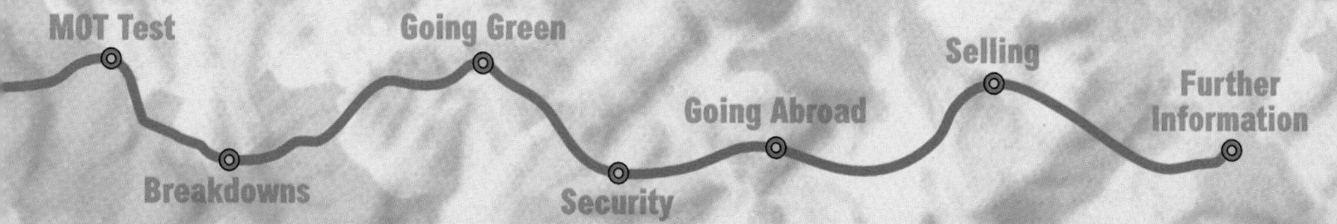

MOT Test
Going Green
Selling
Further Information
Going Abroad
Breakdowns
Security

## About this book

Buying a car may be the largest sum of money you have spent on a single item. Would you know what to look for when buying a car, what events you have to deal with once you own it or the steps to take when you sell it on?

The official information is available to you from various sources but it is not often clear which Department or Agency to contact. This book brings together the useful information you need for responsible ownership. An associated website also provides short cuts to related Government sites providing you with a comprehensive guide to owning a car.

Throughout the book you will find guidance to the website giving extra information. At the website you will be given a menu to enable you to get straight to the information you require. However, DETR does not endorse or recommend above any other, products or services found through this facility. All prices quoted are correct at time of going to press and editions of this book are reprinted from time to time, however you can check out the website for the very latest information.



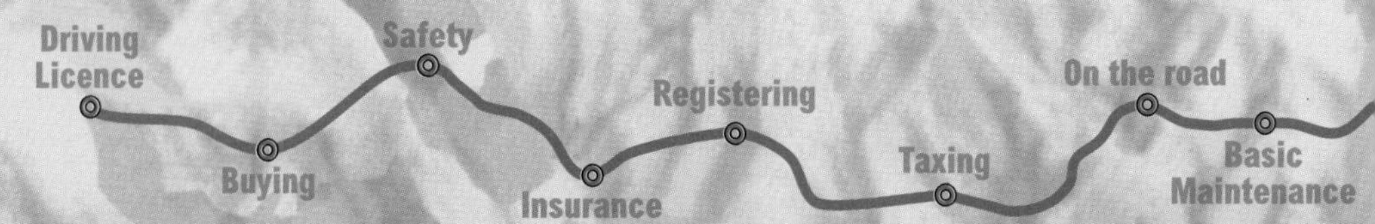

## How to use this book with the website

Throughout this book you will see page tabs offering you more information through the website.

For example, if you are reading chapter six and you would like further information about taxing your car

1 Log onto the website **www.owning-a-car.gov.uk**

2 You will see this home page

3 Choose the section you wish to view, and click on the link in these areas: for example, 'taxing your car'

4 The content area will refresh to show the relevant subject area

5 Click on these links to view related information on Government websites. For example, if you wish to know more about VED bands, click here

6 There is also the opportunity to link to commercial websites. Click here to access these

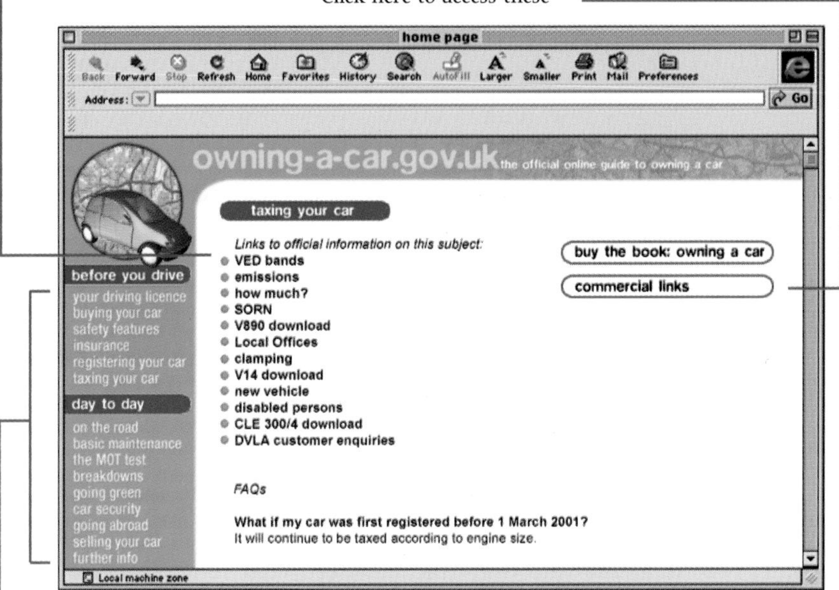


7 To view another section, choose again from the list to the left of the screen.

8 Following one of the official links will take you to a Government website, for example, DVLA.

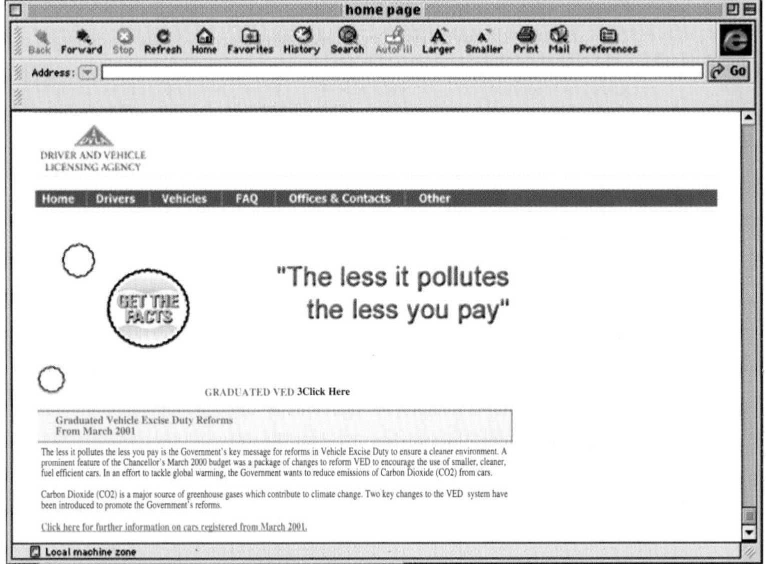

# chapter one

# your driving licence

photocard licences

provisional licence conditions

medical rules

frequently asked questions

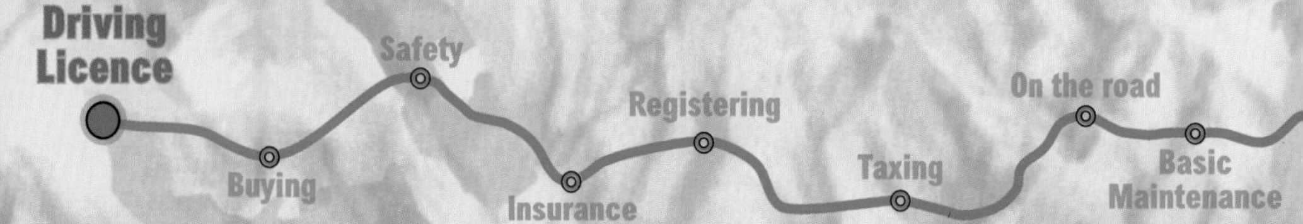

## Photocard driving licences

All driving licences issued by the Driver and Vehicle Licensing Agency (DVLA) are now in photocard format. The photocard driving licence comprises a plastic card containing the photograph, personal information and details of the validity periods and entitlement conveyed by the licence, and a paper counterpart used for recording road traffic offence details and provisional entitlements. The full licence photocard is pink, the provisional photocard is green.

Provisional photocard driving licences also include a red 'L'. Provisional licences issued to addresses in Wales contain a red 'L' and a red 'D' (*dysgwyr* is the Welsh for learner).

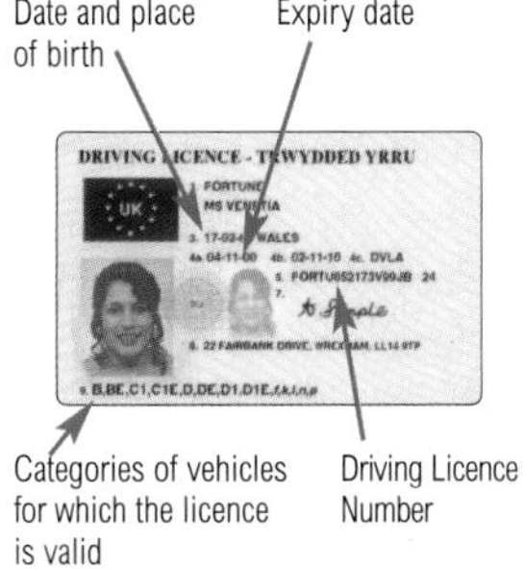


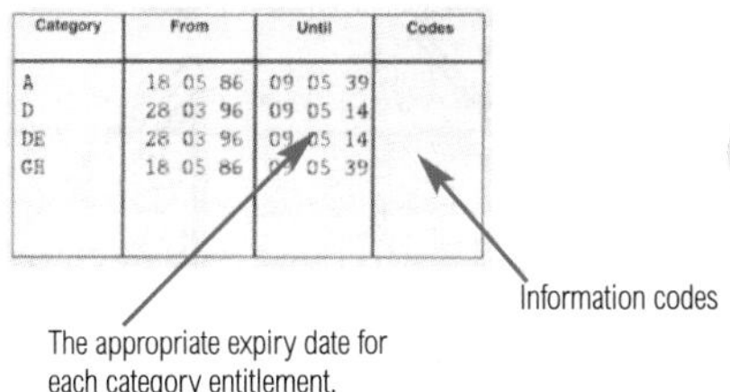

| Category | From | Until | Codes |
|---|---|---|---|
| A | 18 05 86 | 09 05 39 | |
| D | 28 03 96 | 09 05 14 | |
| DE | 28 03 96 | 09 05 14 | |
| CE | 18 05 86 | 09 05 39 | |



The licence consists of two parts, the plastic card and a counterpart which contains further information. Keep these together.

history
how to apply
how much
photocards



MOT Test
Breakdowns
Going Green
Security
Going Abroad
Selling
Further Information

Paper licences held by current drivers will remain valid for the foreseeable future.

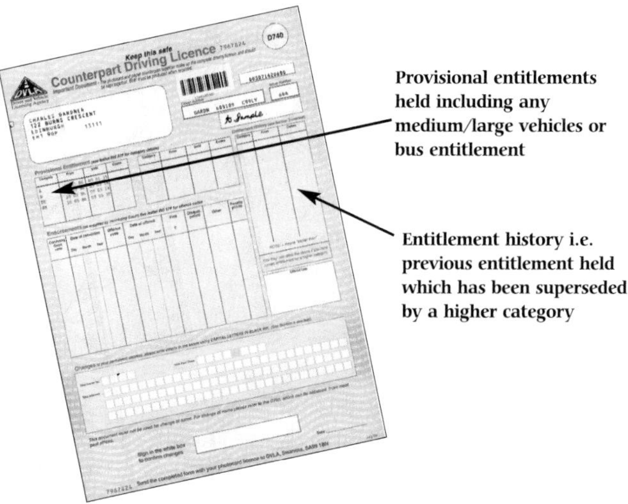


## Now you have your driving licence

As soon as you receive your licence

---

- make a separate note of your driver number. You will need it if you enquire about your driving licence or driver record
- check the details carefully but be aware that if your address is not identical to that shown on your application this may not be an error. DVLA uses the Post Office preferred format.

---

If you find any errors, you must return the licence (both parts) to DVLA for amendment. Take a photocopy and note the date sent.



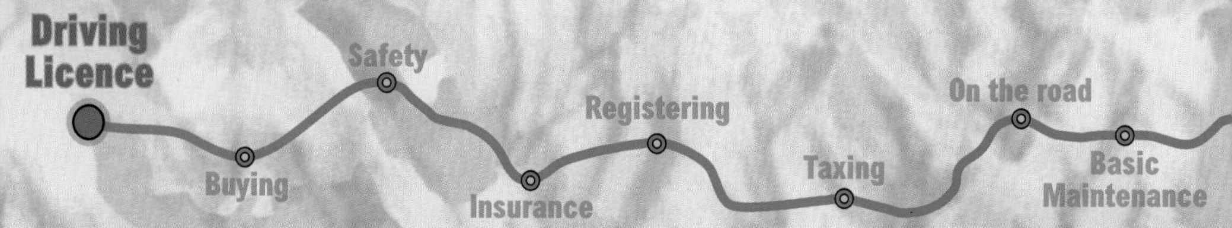

## Provisional licence conditions - cars

While you are learning to drive a car, you must

- be supervised by a qualified driver who is at least 21 years old, and has held (and still holds) a full car driving licence, for at least three years.
- display 'L' plates to the front and rear of the vehicle. Only in Wales can drivers opt to carry 'D' plates only or both 'D' and 'L' plates simultaneously.

adding a test pass

### Growing entitlement

If you are 16 years old, you are not entitled to drive a car unless you are receiving Disability Living Allowance. A licence for a moped may be issued at age 16 and this will 'grow with age' so that once you reach your 17th birthday, it will automatically provide provisional entitlement for cars.

## Medical rules

medical rules

You MUST tell DVLA Drivers' Medical Branch, Swansea, SA99 1TU at once if you suffer from any of these conditions:

- an epileptic event (seizure or fit)
- sudden attacks of disabling dizziness
- severe mental handicap



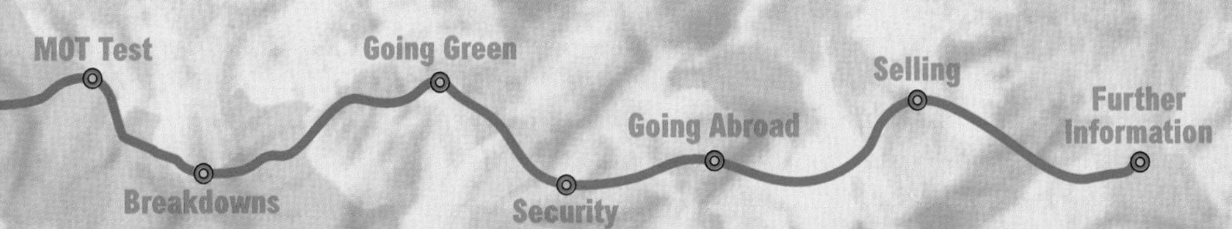

- heart condition requiring a pacemaker, defibrillator or anti-ventricular tachycardia device to be fitted
- diabetes controlled by insulin
- diabetes controlled by tablets
- angina (heart pain) if easily provoked by driving
- Parkinson's disease
- any other chronic neurological condition
- a serious problem with memory
- serious episodes of confusion
- a major or minor stroke
- any type of brain surgery or brain tumour
- severe head injury involving hospital treatment
- any severe psychiatric illness or mental disorder
- continuing/permanent difficulty in the use of the arms or legs which affects your ability to control your vehicle
- persistent misuse of alcohol, illicit drugs or chemical substances in the past three years (do not include drink/driving offences)
- any visual disability which affects both eyes (do not declare short/long sight, colour blindness).



## Drinking and driving

The current legal limit for driving in the UK is 80 mg of alcohol per 100 ml of blood. There is no failsafe guide as to how much you can drink and stay under the current limit. The amount and type of alcoholic drink, and your weight, sex, age and metabolism will all play their part. If you drink and drive you could face a large fine, a period of



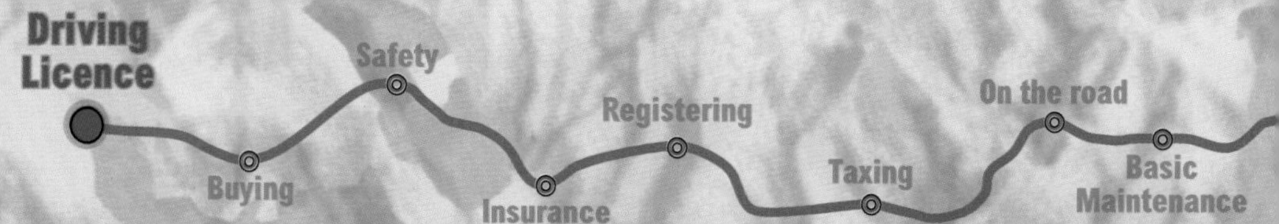

disqualification and possible imprisonment. There are other consequences:

- criminal record
- possible loss of livelihood
- increased insurance costs
- difficulty in hiring a car
- legal expenses
- loss of personal transport and increased travel expenses
- effect on family life
- living with the knowledge that your irresponsibility has caused death, injury or severe distress to innocent people.

## Frequently asked questions

### What do I do if my licence is lost or stolen?

duplicates

You should first notify the police, then apply for a duplicate licence by sending a completed D1 application form (available from most Post Offices) with the appropriate fee and any remaining part of the driving licence to DVLA.

### How do I apply for a renewal when my licence expires?

photocards

The photograph on your licence must be renewed every ten years but your entitlement does not expire. DVLA will send you a renewal reminder shortly before the validity of your



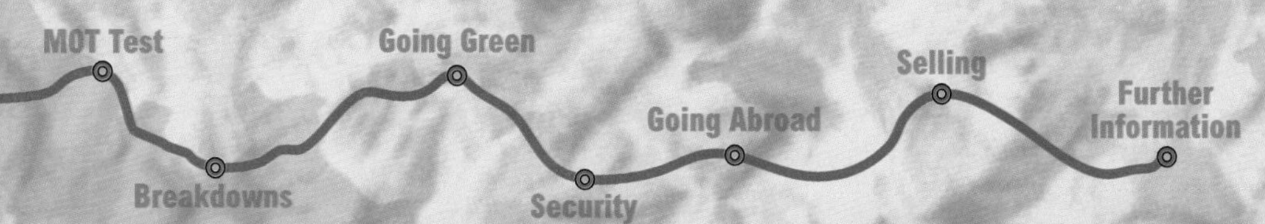

photograph is due to expire. Should you need to change your photograph before the 10 year renewal period you should send a completed D750 form (available from most Post Offices) with the new photograph to DVLA.

change of address

### How do I notify DVLA of a change of name and/or address?

It is a legal requirement to notify DVLA of any changes and failure to comply could cost the driver a £1,000 fine. For a change of address only, you should complete the relevant section on the counterpart and return both parts of the licence. For change of name, you would need to complete a D750 and provide evidence of the change (e.g. marriage certificate or deed poll).

### Is it necessary to notify DVLA of a deceased driver?

Yes. The person dealing with the effects of the deceased person should return both parts of the licence to DVLA with a covering letter.

vocational licence

### Can I drive a minibus on my car licence?

If you had entitlement to drive cars before 1 January 1997 – group A (B for automatics) on old style licences or category B and D1 not for hire or reward on new style licences – you can drive a minibus provided you are aged 21 or over, the minibus has a maximum of 16 passenger seats and is not being used for hire or reward.



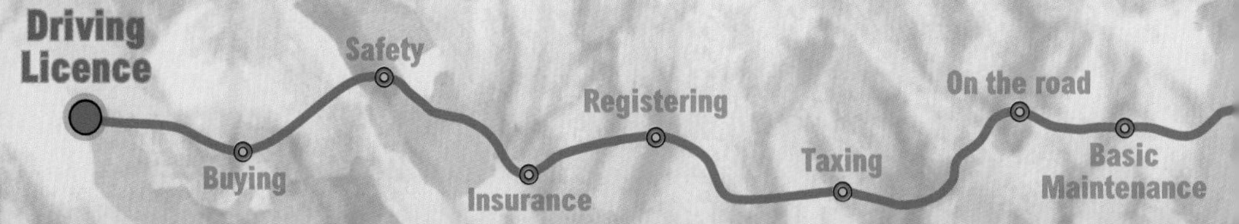

To drive a minibus which has over eight passenger seats for hire or reward you will normally need passenger carrying vehicle (PCV) entitlement, category D1 or D. To obtain this you must meet higher medical standards and take a further driving test.

From 1 January 1998, your minibus entitlement will remain valid in the UK and on temporary visits abroad until your licence is next renewed. When this happens your minibus entitlement (D1, D1+E not for hire or reward) can only be issued if you make a special application which will involve meeting higher medical standards.

In general, car licences have to be renewed when drivers reach the age of 70. Younger drivers with restricted medical licences will also be affected by the new rules, when their licences are renewed.

If your car licence does not allow you to drive minibuses, there are certain circumstances where you may still be able to do so. You may drive a minibus with up to 16 passenger seats provided

- you drive on behalf of a non-commercial body for social purposes, but not for hire or reward
- you are aged 21 or over
- you have held a car licence for at least two years
- you are providing your services on a voluntary basis
- the minibus weight is no more than 3.5 tonnes excluding any specialist equipment for the carriage of disabled passengers, or no more than 4.25 tonnes in certain circumstances

• you are able to meet the health standards for driving a D1 vehicle, if you are aged 70 or over.

---

When driving a minibus under these conditions you may not receive any payment other than out of pocket expenses, or tow any size trailer; you may only drive minibuses in the UK. Drivers age 70 or over will need to make a special application which involves meeting higher medical standards.

**NOTE**: **ALL PERMIT MINIBUS DRIVERS**: you cannot take a permit minibus abroad if it is used for hire or reward unless you hold either PCV D1 or D entitlement.

## Can I drive a bus?

If you wish to drive buses with more than 16 passenger seats you must obtain category D entitlement. To do this you must submit an application for provisional category D entitlement and take a theory test and a practical driving test in a bus which meets test requirements. You will need to pass a test and obtain a category D licence before trying a test for D + E entitlement.

towing

## I have just passed my test and want to tow a small trailer; can I do this?

You must pass a test in a car before you can take a test in most other categories. Also, if you wish to tow a heavy trailer you must first pass a test in the associated rigid vehicle.



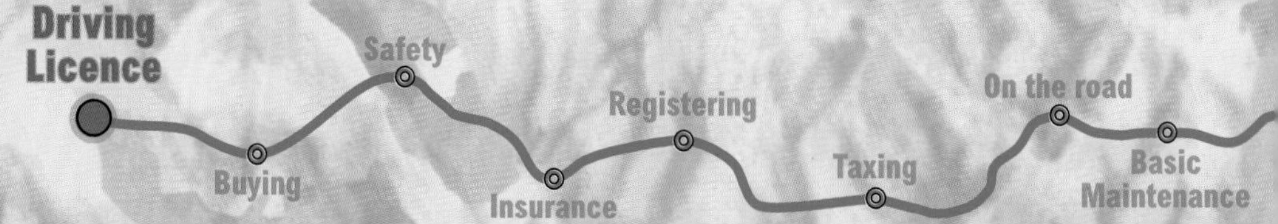

Learner drivers in categories B, C1, C, D1 and D cannot tow a trailer until they have passed a test with a trailer.

endorsements

**I was stopped for speeding and the Police Officer took my licence. I presume I will have my licence endorsed – how long does it stay on my licence?**

Endorsements remain on a (counterpart) licence for

- 11 years from date of conviction for offences relating to drink/drugs and driving, causing death by careless driving whilst under the influence of drink/drugs, and causing death by careless driving then failing to provide a specimen for analysis
- four years from date of conviction for reckless/dangerous driving and offences resulting in disqualification
- four years from the date of offence in all other cases.

At the appropriate time, you can apply to remove your endorsement(s) from your licence by completing a D1 application form available from post offices. (The photocard and counterpart should also be returned). There will be a charge and the form will tell you how much to pay.

New Drivers Act

**I've heard that I can lose my licence if I get six penalty points. Is this true?**

Yes it is. The 'New Drivers Act' means that if you reach six or more penalty points within two years of passing your test

(the probationary period), DVLA will automatically revoke your licence on being notified by a court or fixed penalty office. You will then have to surrender your full licence and obtain a provisional licence, drive as a learner, and pass the theory and practical tests again in order to regain your full driving licence.

There is no appeal against such automatic revocation. The only appeal available is against the conviction for which the penalty points were awarded; the court will be able to advise you on the process if you believe you have a case. If you do make such an appeal, once the court notifies DVLA the revocation will be suspended until the outcome of the appeal.

Penalty points counting towards the total of six include any you incurred before passing the test, as long as the offence took place not more than three years before the latest penalty point offence.

Points imposed after the probationary period will also count if the offence was committed during that period. If you accept a fixed penalty notice you cannot appeal.

Passing the retest will not remove the penalty points from your licence, and if the total reaches 12, you are liable to be disqualified by a court.

## Can I use my UK licence abroad?



If you are visiting, you can use your full UK licence to drive throughout the European Community (EC) and European Economic Area (EEA) member states. If you want to drive elsewhere, contact any motoring organisation for advice on International Driving Permits (IDPs). To get an IDP you must be over 18, resident in the UK and have passed a driving test.

If you are planning to live abroad, your licence will be recognised in all EC/EEA member states but you should check with the driver licensing authorities of the country you are moving to, whether within or outside the EEA, for information about driving there once you become a resident.

## How do I tell DVLA about a medical condition?

If you are completing a form D1 you can tell DVLA about your condition in the health section. If you already have a licence, write to:

**Drivers' Medical Unit**
DVLA
Swansea
SA99 1TU

with

- your driver number, or your full name and date of birth
- details of your medical condition in as much detail as possible.

You must tell DVLA if you have any of the previously listed conditions. Otherwise you are committing an offence that can lead to prosecution and a fine of up to £1000.

A person who knowingly makes a false statement for the purpose of obtaining a driving licence is liable to a fine of up to £2500.

## What happens when I tell DVLA about a medical condition?

They will send you a medical questionnaire which asks for your permission to let a medical adviser get reports from your doctor and specialists.



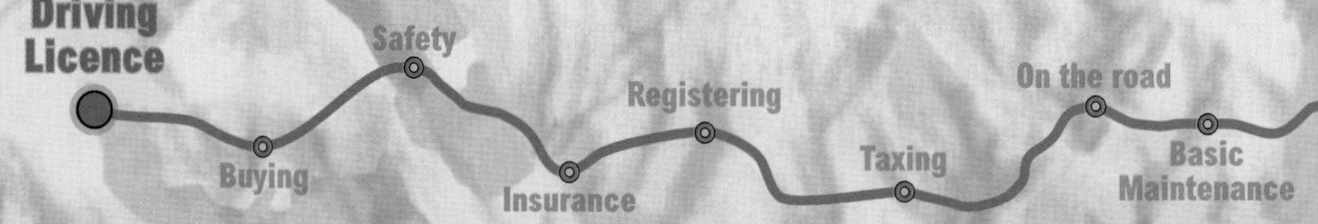

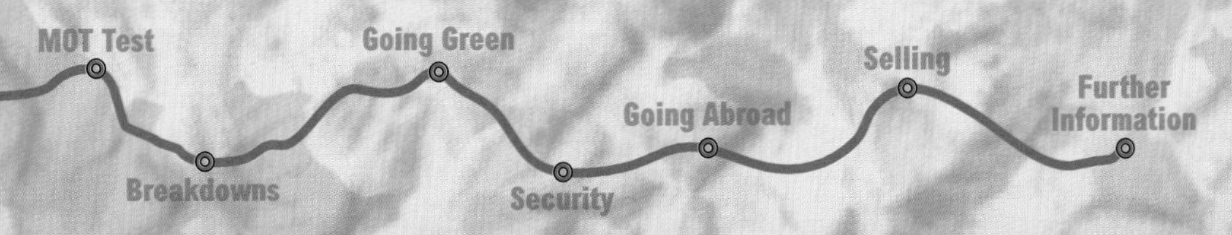
MOT Test
Breakdowns
Going Green
Security
Going Abroad
Selling
Further Information

chapter two

# buying your car

before you buy
running costs
recalls
paying for your car
buying from – a dealer
– an auction
– privately
choosing safety
buying a car from abroad
frequently asked questions

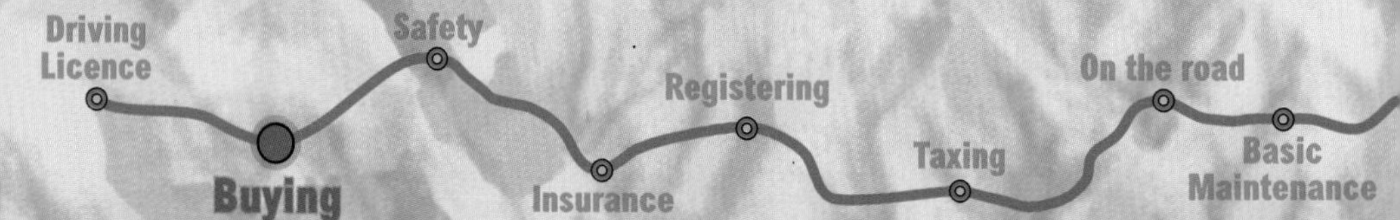

## Before you buy

There are several things to consider before you decide which car you want to buy. It may be useful to make a checklist to help you choose.

DVLA Register details

Ask yourself:

- do I really need a car at all? It may be cheaper to use public transport and hire a vehicle periodically for individual journeys. This will save the cost of repairs, servicing, insurance and parking costs while helping to reduce air pollution and traffic congestion
- if I buy a car will I use it for
  - long journeys
  - carrying passengers
  - short journeys in urban areas
  - parking in confined spaces
  - carrying sports equipment or large objects?

Think of your practical needs and your financial ceiling. Visit as many showrooms as you can and discuss your needs with the sales people.

Capital outlay will only give you ownership of the car and will not help towards the running costs.

emissions

New cars are taxed on their carbon dioxide ($CO_2$) emission figure and the type of fuel they use. So you could save money whilst doing your bit for the environment (see chapter 11). Check out the emissions table for new cars on the website.

## Running costs

Ask family and friends about the cost of running their cars. You need to think about

- servicing
- fuel consumption
- spares and/or repairs
- depreciation
- insurance
- tyres
- tax.



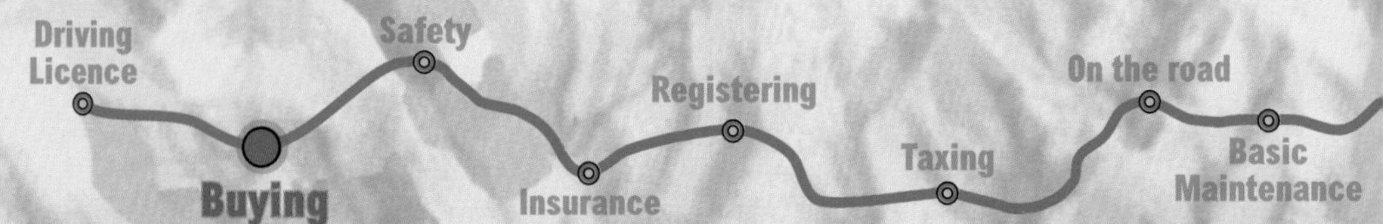

For example

A small engined car will do as much as 67.5 miles per gallon but it is not practical if you want to carry five passengers, nor is it suitable for off road use.

Visit your newsagent who will have a selection of magazines available to help you choose. These show road tests and comprehensive price guides. They can also tell you about any changes in model or specification which could affect the price. There are useful guides to insurance groups which can vary from car to car depending on its value and power output.

There are also several websites which will help you.

## Recalls



From time to time motor manufacturers recall their cars for modification. These can be for minor adjustments to the cosmetic make up of the car, or could be a potential safety hazard. You should ensure that if a car has been recalled, the previous owner has had the work completed. Ask to see repair bills and the service history of the vehicle.



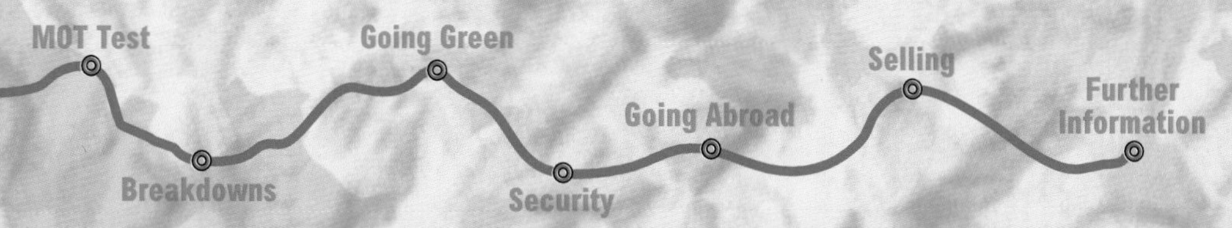

## Paying for your car

If you intend to borrow money to purchase your car ensure you receive professional advice. Borrowing more than you can afford could result in the car being repossessed by a loan company, leaving you with nothing but stress.

Make sure the vehicle you want to buy is not

- stolen
- subject to outstanding finance
- seriously damaged.

Note: An MOT certificate is not a guarantee that the car is roadworthy. The test only relates to the condition of the testable items at the time of the test.

SEE NOTES OVERLEAF
TEST CERTIFICATE
Vehicle Inspectorate
KEEP THIS CERTIFICATE IN A SAFE PLACE
Vehicle colour
Vehicle make
Date of issue
Date of expiry
VT20
Authentication Stamp
WARNING
CHECK
THE MOT HOTLINE



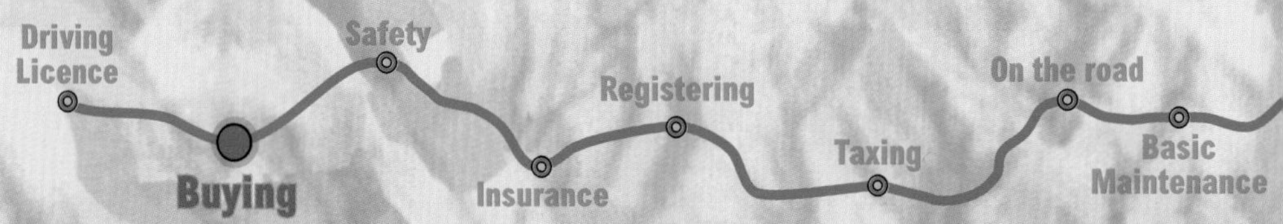

# Buying your car

## Buying from a dealer

consumer advice

used vehicles

code of practice

The law gives you protection when you buy a car. The vehicle must be of a satisfactory quality. That means that it must meet the standard a responsible person would regard as acceptable - bearing in mind its description and the price asked. This covers the finish of the car, its safety and durability. The vehicle must be free from defects unless they are pointed out by the seller. If the vehicle is inspected on your behalf, the dealer is not liable for any faults that should have been identified. Get a description of the vehicle's condition from the dealer and ask whether there is a pre-sale inspection checklist.

## Buying from an auction

auctions

Decide how much you want to spend before you go, and stick to it. Go as a spectator first to see what happens. Take along someone who knows about cars. Each vehicle has a form attached to the windscreen giving you an

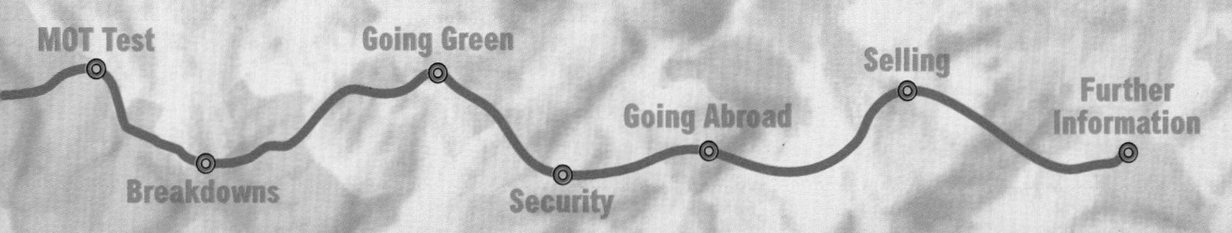

idea of the vehicle's background. Be careful: many cars are 'sold as seen' which diminishes your statutory rights if the vehicle turns out to be faulty.

buying privately

## Buying privately

This is potentially more risky than buying from a dealer. The car may be stolen or have outstanding finance. Watch out for

- adverts that give mobile phone numbers or specify a time to call
- the same phone number appearing in several ads
- a seller who wants to bring the vehicle to you.

Ask to see the registration document and check the details against the vehicle. The document will also show the number of previous keepers. Having the document is not proof of legal ownership. Make sure the seller gives you a signed and dated receipt. It should indicate the selling price (including any deposit) and that you have paid 'in full'.

# Choosing safety

When choosing a car, you should look for the safety features described in chapter 3. You may also want to consult other information about the model you are interested in. Statistical information about the risk of injury in accidents



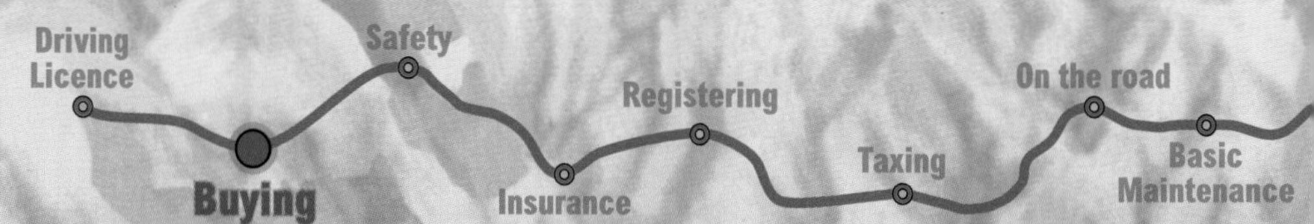

for different makes and models of car is published each year in *Transport Statistics Great Britain*. The results of Euro NCAP crash tests carried out on some of the most popular new models in Europe are available from:

NCAP tests

- Euro NCAP, (telephone +32 2 286 8040)
- the AIT-FIA European Bureau (telephone +32 2 282 08 16)
- from the AA website.

They are also published from time to time by motoring magazines, such as *What Car?*, and the Consumers' Association.

## Buying a car from abroad

importing a car

There is a substantial amount of paperwork involved in buying and registering a new or second hand car from abroad. You may want to consider using an agent to deal with this administration for you.

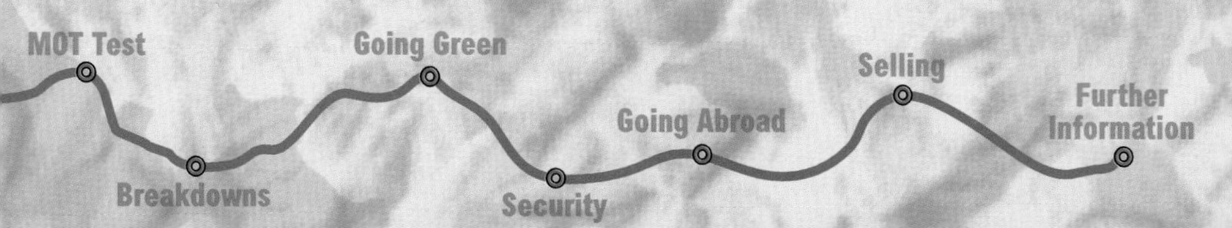

A permanently imported vehicle must

- comply with the relevant construction and use requirements
- be registered immediately if it is used or kept on the road
- be notified to HM Customs within seven days of arrival in Great Britain.

## Pre-registration formalities

type approval

For most new vehicles, you must produce evidence from the manufacturer or supplier that the vehicle is type-approved. In the case of a car this usually means the certificate of conformity. Such certificates will need to stipulate that the vehicle is suitable for use in left-hand traffic and/or has a speedometer marked in miles per hour.

## Non-approved vehicles

For vehicles not subject to type approval, a vehicle must undergo a technical inspection.

roadworthiness

Generally, a vehicle up to 10 years old is likely to require single vehicle approval, which establishes that it meets the required design and construction standards. Vehicles over three years old will also need to pass the standard MOT roadworthiness test.

For details about registering an imported vehicle see chapter 5.



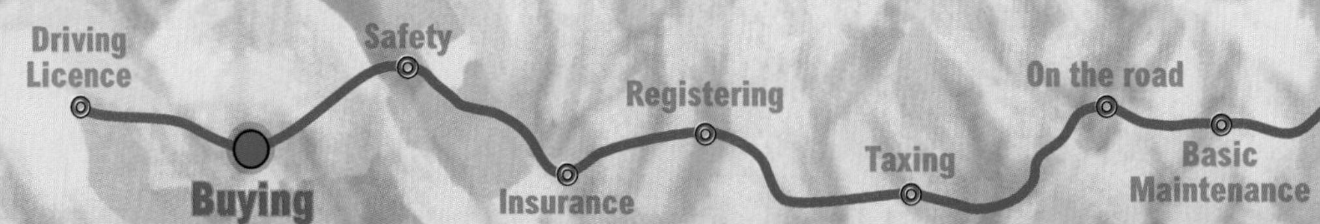

## Frequently asked questions

### I have no mechanical knowledge. How can I protect myself?

consumer advice

Ask friends or relatives to recommend an established firm. Members of the Retail Motor Industry Federation and the Scottish Trade Association subscribe to a code of practice supported by the Office of Fair Trading. Some dealers get their cars part inspected by the AA or RAC – ask to see the report. Inspect the vehicle yourself, or have it inspected by a knowledgeable friend or relative. Better still, you can have it inspected by an independent organisation such as the AA or RAC.

code of practice

### What is 'cut and shut'?

Sometimes, two damaged cars are cut in half and the 'good' halves welded together to create a new one. These are known as 'cut and shuts'. It is not easy to tell when this has happened, but unless the work has been done to a very high standard, the resulting vehicle is very likely to be unsafe. Cut and shuts should be treated with extreme caution and should be subject to a thorough examination. There are companies which can tell you whether a car is an insurance company write-off, although they will charge you for this service.

write-off?



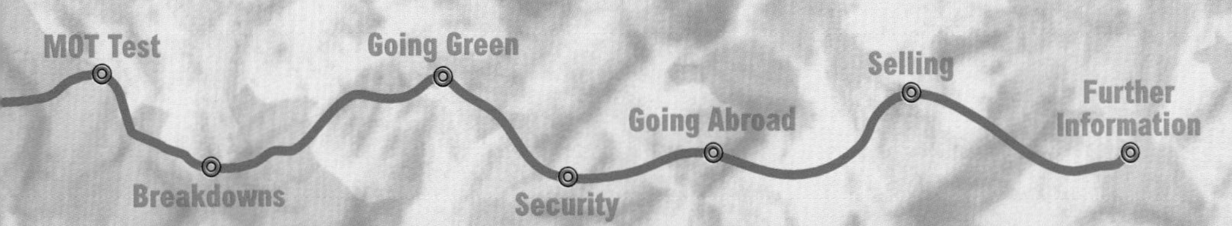

## How do I know that the seller actually owns the vehicle?

whose car?

A car bought on hire purchase or conditional sale belongs to the finance company until the loan has been repaid. Before buying, check with a company that keeps databases of information about cars to see whether the one you are thinking of buying is clear. If you are buying from a dealer, ask whether this check has already been carried out.

DVLA advice

## How can I avoid buying a stolen vehicle?

If you buy a stolen vehicle the police can take it away and return it to the legal owner or insurance company, even if you have bought it in good faith. Never buy a car without seeing the registration document. Check it thoroughly

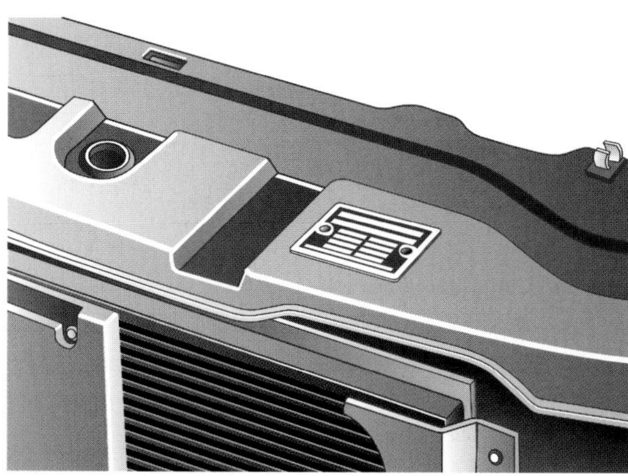



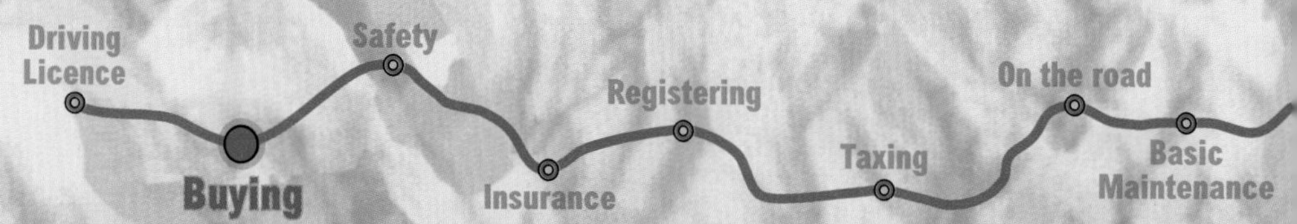

against the vehicle: do the details on the registration document and the vehicle identification numbers (VIN) correspond? The VIN can be found on a metal plate in the engine compartment and stamped in the bodywork under the driver's seat. Some vehicles also have a VIN etched into the lamps and windows.

Ask the seller to show you something other than the registration document such as a driving licence or a utility bill bearing their name and address. Also

- check the windscreen and windows for scratches or stickers to cover up etching
- ask to see insurance and MOT certificates
- check the VIN and engine numbers to see if they have been tampered with.

## How do I know if the mileage is accurate?

Try to find out the vehicle's history. Past MOT certificates and the service documents will show mileage information. Some traders have access to specialist databases to run their own mileage checks. Ask whether a check has recently been undertaken.

Watch out for

- low mileage, but heavy wear and tear
- pedal rubbers, steering wheel and gear lever knobs which are either very worn or have been replaced

• mileometer digits that do not align correctly
• worn upholstery and carpets.

---

**I bought a car that has given me nothing but trouble, and now I have discovered it was involved in a major accident. What can I do?**

Go back to the seller straight away, explain the problem and say what you want done.

trading standards

citizens advice

If you aren't happy with the outcome, get advice. Contact your local Trading Standards Service (sometimes called Consumer Protection Department) – their address is in the phone book under your local council or, in Northern Ireland, the Department of Economic Development. Or go to a Citizens Advice Bureau or consumer advice centre – see the phone book for details.

If a dealer is a member, one of the trade associations listed opposite may be able to help. There is a code of practice for dealing with complaints.

You can go to court or use a trade association conciliation/arbitration scheme. A consumer adviser can explain the procedure.



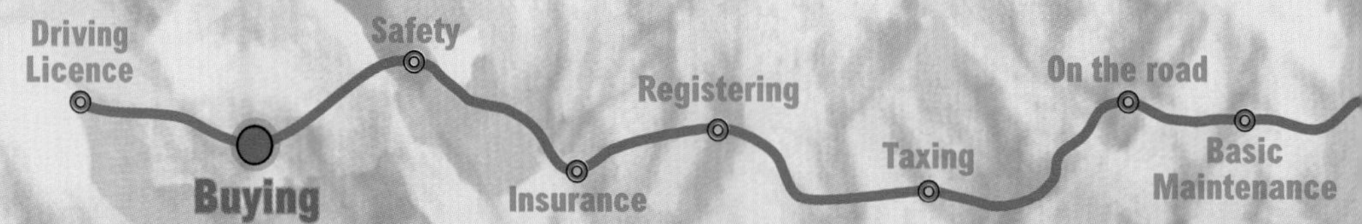

If you are a member of the AA or RAC, they will help if you have problems with buying a used car. Some useful phone numbers are:

AA: 0990 500 600

RAC: 0990 533 533

**Office of Fair Trading Consumer Information Line**

For guidance on where practical help may be obtained if problems arise in the purchase of goods and services:
Tel: 0345 22 44 99 (calls charged at local rates)

For complaints about used cars and repairs/servicing in England, Wales and Northern Ireland:

RMIF

**The National Conciliation Service**
**Retail Motor Industry Federation (RMIF)**
2nd Floor, Chestnut House
9 North Street, Rugby CV21 2AB
Tel: RMIF Motorline 0345 585350

For complaints about used cars and repairs/servicing in Scotland:

SMTA

**Customer Complaints Service**
**Scottish Motor Trade Association Ltd**
3 Palmerston Place, Edinburgh EH12 5AF
Tel: 0131 225 3643



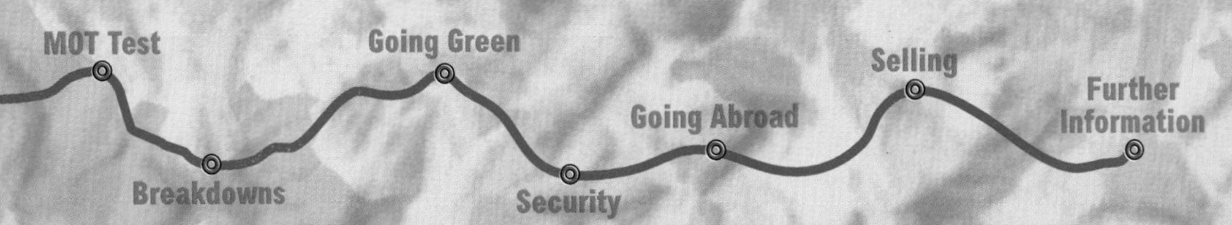

For complaints about cars still under a manufacturer's warranty:

SMMT

**The Consumer Relations Adviser**
**Society of Motor Manufacturers and Traders**
Forbes House, Halkin Street
London SW1X TDS
Tel: 020 7235 7000

For information about a car's history:

HPI Check: 01722 422422

data check

AA Car Data Check: 0800 234999

Currently, these are the two companies which provide information on whether a car is an insurance company write-off or belongs to a finance company. They may also have mileage information. Check motoring magazines and the Internet to see whether any new companies have been set up.



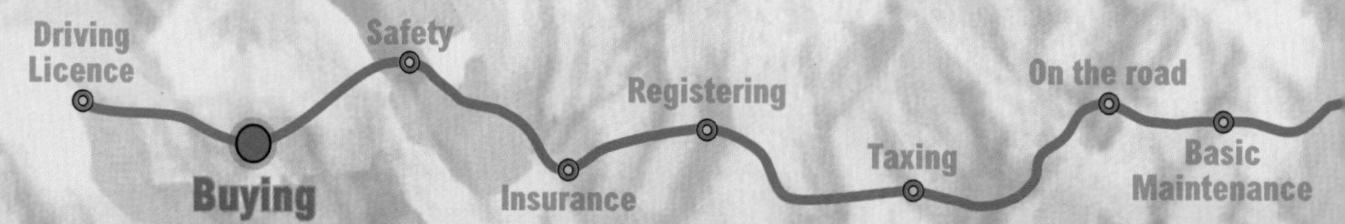

FOR
SALE



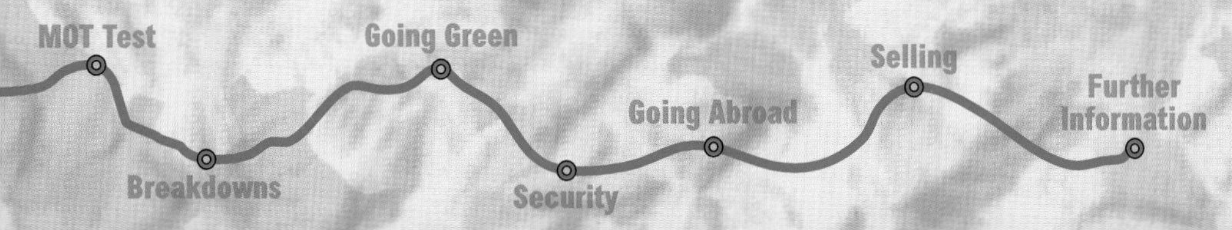
MOT Test
Breakdowns
Going Green
Security
Going Abroad
Selling
Further Information

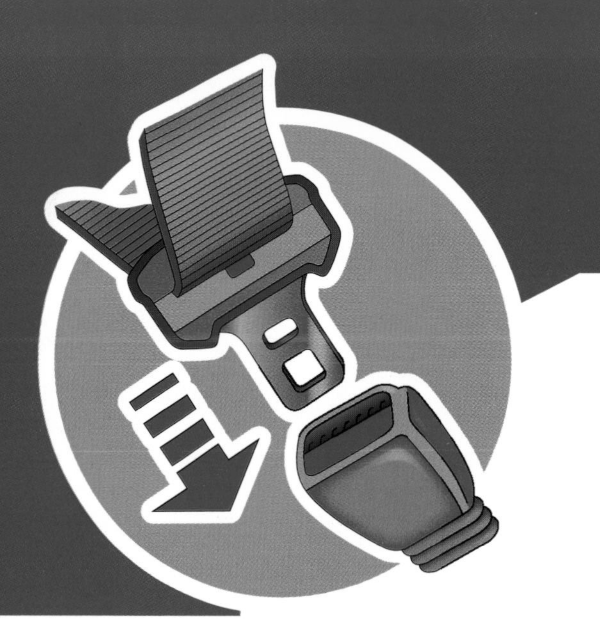

chapter three

# safety features

think about safety

car structure

primary safety

secondary safety

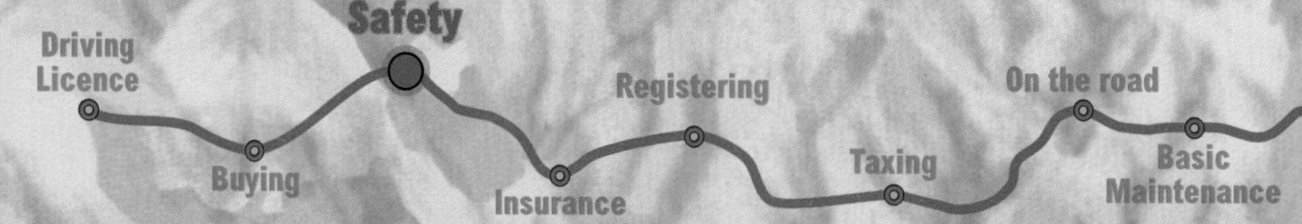

## Think about safety

All new models of car are tested to ensure that they comply with European legislation before the manufacturer is allowed to sell them to the public. These regulations are detailed and are primarily concerned with standards of safety, both to help drivers avoid accidents (primary safety) and also to ensure that cars protect people when crashes do occur (secondary safety).

code of practice

NCAP Tests

Many cars are designed to have a safety performance which exceeds these levels and they may also have additional safety features.

Growing consumer interest in safety and constantly improving regulations have played a major part in influencing car manufacturers. This in turn ensures safer cars.

All drivers make mistakes, but choosing a safer car can prevent that mistake becoming an accident or reduce the seriousness of the accident (primary safety features). Choosing a safer car can also reduce the severity of injuries you may suffer if an accident happens (secondary safety features).

accident research

Primary safety features such as good tyres, brakes, suspension, lights, visibility and ergonomics can greatly help a driver avoid hazards. Secondary safety features such as good frontal impact protection, side impact protection, pedestrian protection, seat belts and airbags can greatly



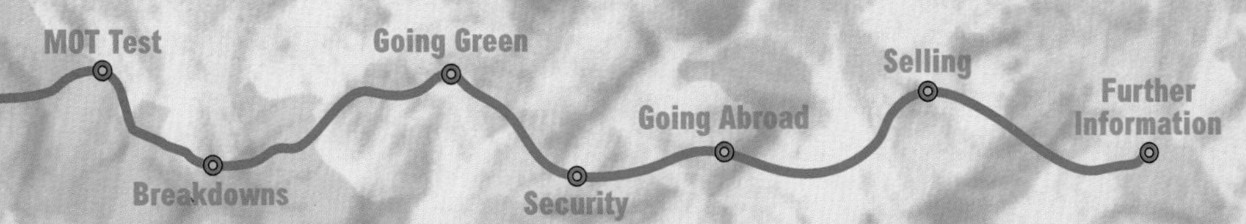

reduce the risk of death or injury to car occupants and pedestrians.

Below are some safety features that are worth checking before deciding which car to buy.

vehicle standards

tyres

| **primary safety** (accident avoidance) | **Secondary safety** (reducing injury risk) |
|---|---|
| • tyres/brakes | • frontal impact protection |
| • anti-lock braking system (ABS) | • side impact protection |
| • traction control system | • seat belt pre-tensioners and webbing grabbers |
| • well laid-out controls | • airbags |
| • stability | • head restraints |
| • good lamps | • steering wheel design |
| • good visibility for the driver | |

vehicle safety

## Car structure

Driver error is still the main cause of accidents.

However, a car's structure has a key role in reducing the severity of occupant injuries in a crash. The aim is to have parts of the car which can absorb as much of the impact energy as possible, while having a strong protected area for the occupants which will retain its shape. When a new model is being developed, the designer has to take into account how real structures behave and deform in crashes in order to identify structural features which are likely to improve the chances of the occupants surviving.



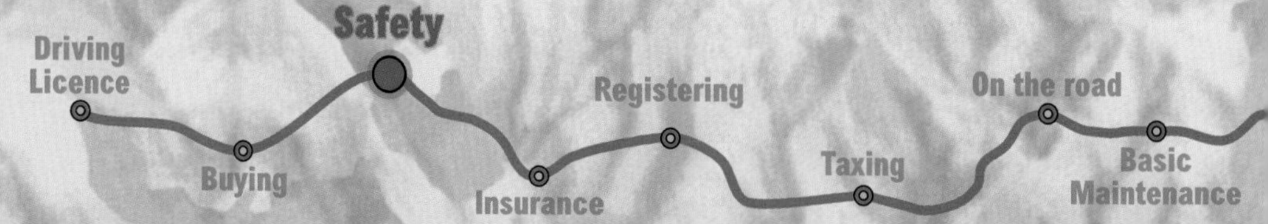

Secondary safety features, such as seat belts, airbags and head restraints, can further significantly reduce the risk or severity of injury in the event of an accident (see chapter 7 under 'seat belts' for more information about what happens in a crash).

## Primary safety

### Controls and visibility

A comfortable driving position is also an important factor to bear in mind when choosing a new car. This will help to reduce fatigue and enable you to maintain concentration. So try out the driver's seat before purchasing, and go for a test drive.

You need to be able to reach and work the pedals to have full control of your car, but you also need to be as far as practical from the steering wheel. Keeping away from the steering wheel and column reduces the risk of impact injuries to your face and head in an accident. This is important whether or not the car has an airbag.



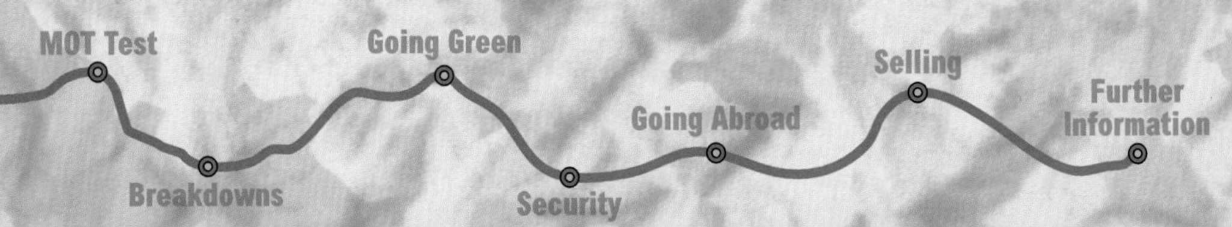

Can you see all the important dials when you sit in the car? Can you see all you need to see out of the windows or do the pillars restrict your lines of sight?

Try the minor controls to see if they are easy to reach and use without needing to take your eyes off the road or move in your seat.

Work the heating and demisting features and try to judge if they will do their job well. Think about cooling and fresh air ventilation, especially face level vents which help prevent motorway fatigue.

When you take the car for a test drive to make sure you are happy with the visibility and controls while the car is moving.

## Anti-lock braking system (ABS)

Many cars have ABS fitted or it is available as an option. ABS employs wheel speed sensors to anticipate when a wheel is about to lock under extreme braking. Just before this happens the system releases the brakes momentarily before automatically reapplying them. This cycle is repeated several times a second to maximise braking performance, sending a pulsating sensation through the brake pedal. You may find this a little disconcerting the first time it occurs and you may be tempted to respond by relaxing the pressure on the brake pedal. However it is important that maximum pressure is maintained.

To activate the ABS the driver must apply maximum pedal effort. This pressure must be maintained until the vehicle has stopped or the hazard has been safely avoided. Reducing the pedal pressure or pumping the brake pedal will reduce the effectiveness of the system.

ABS does not necessarily reduce your stopping distance, but because the wheels are prevented from locking, you can continue to steer – something that you would not be able to do if the wheels were locked. On snow, gravel or other loose surfaces a vehicle with a conventional braking system may stop in a shorter distance; however, the vehicle with ABS will maintain steering control.



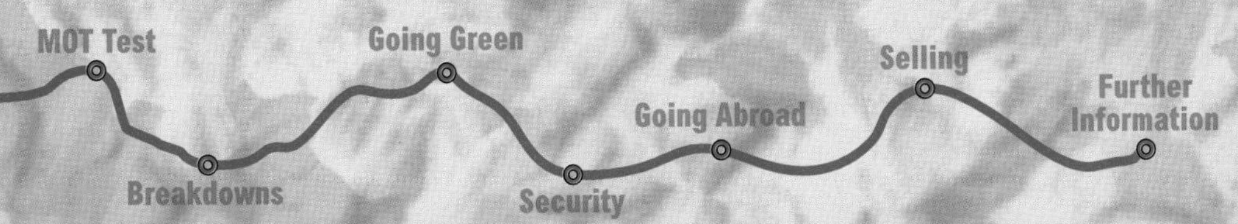

ABS is only a driver aid. It doesn't remove the need for good driving practice such as anticipating events and assessing road conditions.

Cars with ABS have a dashboard light, which illuminates momentarily when the car is initially started, to confirm that certain checks have been satisfactorily completed. When a fault has been detected the warning light remains on. The car should not been driven until repaired.

## Traction control system

Traction control systems may be incorporated into vehicles fitted with ABS. In slippery conditions, such as ice or snow, it is often difficult to accelerate in any car without the wheels spinning. Traction control systems prevent wheelspin by controlling the accelerator and/or automatically applying the brake of the spinning wheel to produce a smooth take-up of drive. Traction control is an aid to primary safety by helping to keep the car under control.

## Four-wheel drive (4WD)

In slippery conditions or on off-road surfaces, it is obviously helpful if all the wheels can be used to get the power from the engine onto the ground. Four wheel drive allows all the wheels to drive and improves primary safety by making the most of the grip that the tyres have on the road. It has some



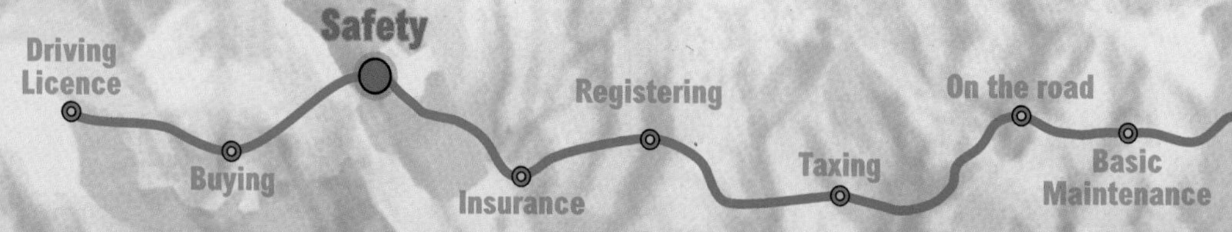

benefits for all types of vehicles, but its major use is on off-road vehicles such as Range Rovers, etc.

## Stability

The stability of a vehicle is a compromise between features such as comfort, acceleration, braking and cornering performance. In general, the normal family car which is low to the ground with a wheel close to each corner will be more stable than the typically taller, off-road type of vehicle. These normally have a high centre of gravity, short wheelbase and narrow track to suit lower speed off-road driving and should be driven with greater care when used on normal roads.

Increasing numbers of cars are also being fitted with stability control systems which electronically control the Anti-lock braking (ABS) and the accelerator to improve stability by reducing the possibility of skidding during cornering or manoeuvres to avoid obstacles. Such vehicles will have the full integrated electronic package of ABS, traction control and stability control.

## Lights

Lights on vehicles are an essential safety feature, as they help the driver to see the road ahead and show other road users the location of the vehicle.

Consideration needs to be given to the maintenance, installation and use of lights as they can cause dazzle to other road users, which could lead to an accident (see chapters 7 and 8)

## Fog lamps and driving lamps

Front fog lamps or driving lamps do not have to be fitted, but they may provide some benefits in certain circumstances.



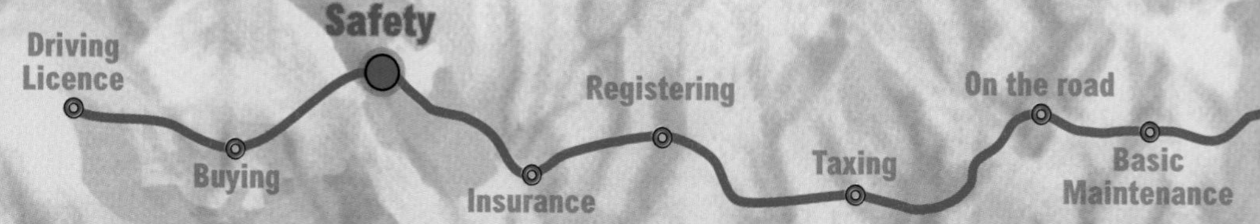

### Brake lights

Research has shown that separate (as opposed to combined) brake lights and rear position lamps – as on some models – can help following drivers respond more quickly to brake signals. There are similar advantages in having a third brake light located away from the other rear lights, usually mounted centrally and fairly high up.

## Secondary safety



### Inertia reel seat belts

Modern three-point lap and diagonal seat belts have an inertia reel mechanism. This normally allows the belt to be pulled out of the reel, but when a vehicle is slowed by hard braking or in a crash, 'inertia' locks the seat belt reel automatically. Inertia reel seat belts usually have a second mechanism which locks when the shoulder belt itself is suddenly jerked. You can test this by tugging sharply on the belt.



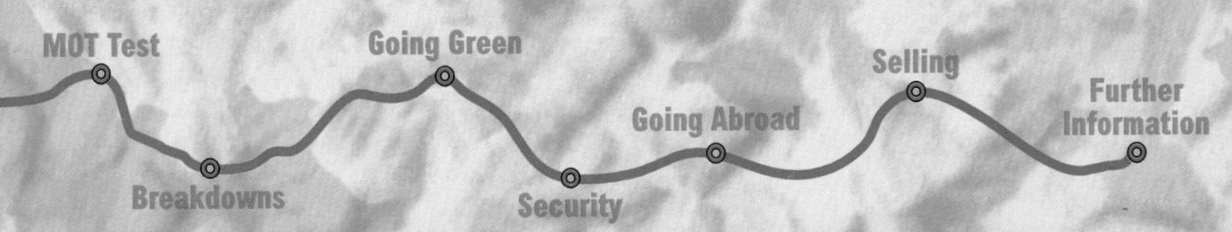

### Pre-tensioners, webbing grabbers and load limiters

Many models have 'pre-tensioners' and/or 'webbing grabbers' on the front seat belts to reduce the slack.

Pre-tensioners tighten belts during the first milliseconds of a crash, before you start to move. Webbing grabbers clamp the belt webbing just outside the reel, preventing more coming out. These two features, separately or preferably together, reduce the likelihood of you moving forward far enough to hit anything, so increasing your chance of surviving a severe accident.

Some cars equipped with airbags may have load limiters on the front seat belts. Load limiters allow for a controlled amount of forward movement in a severe collision, when the load on the seat belt reaches a certain level. This has the effect of limiting the forces on your chest. As there is an airbag, you should not hit your head on the steering wheel or fascia, despite the increased amount of forward movement.

### Steering wheels and columns

Unless the car is fitted with an airbag, drivers are most likely to be injured in an accident by hitting their face or head on the steering wheel or column.



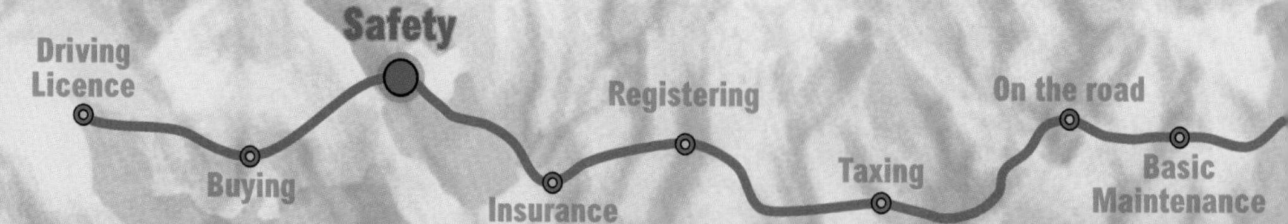

When choosing a car without an airbag, look at the design of the steering wheel. It should allow a good depth of padding over any hard parts in its construction. Avoid steering wheels which don't have substantial padding in the centre or on the rim or have hard objects such as switches where your head or face might hit. All new models are subjected to an original approval process to ensure a minimum level of protection.

## Airbags



Airbags are sometimes referred to as 'supplementary restraint systems' (SRS) as they are designed to improve the protection offered by seat belts. Seat belts should therefore always be worn, whether or not airbags are fitted.

Front airbags operate in a severe frontal collision. Crash sensors detect the sudden reduction in speed and send a signal to the airbag inflator which fills the bag with a gas. Full inflation occurs faster than the blink of an eye. The bag begins to deflate instantly, in a controlled way, to cushion the impact.

Most new cars have a front airbag for the driver as standard equipment. Drivers' airbags improve the protection offered by seat belts in serious frontal crashes.



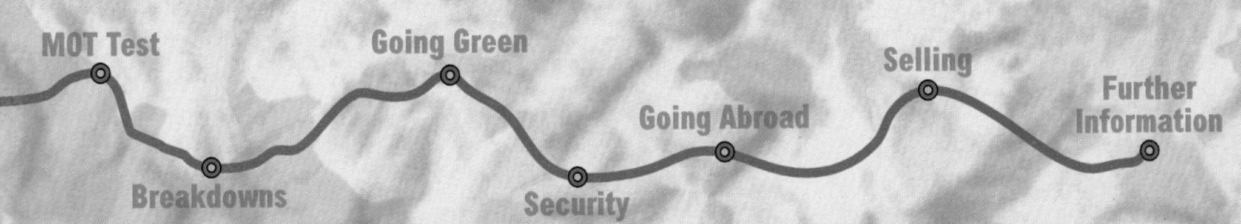

Many new cars are now available with front passenger airbags. There is too little data to draw firm conclusions, but their benefits may be more limited as passengers are at less risk than drivers of hitting the dashboard (see chapter 7).

## Side impact

Look for a car with well padded door panels and armrests which are not next to you when you are sitting normally.

Consider a car with side airbags. These work in a similar manner to front airbags, but are located in either the side structure of the car or the seats. As their name suggests, they are designed to inflate and protect the occupants in a side impact.

The simple addition of a 'side impact bar' to strengthen the door will not necessarily improve your chances of escaping serious internal injury in a full side impact, although it may help in front or glancing impacts by reducing the extent to which the door is pushed into the passenger compartment.

## Bull bars

'Bull bars', also known as 'protection bars', are often fitted on four-wheel drive vehicles and vans. People generally fit them either for purely cosmetic reasons, trying to give a

tough off-road image to vehicles which are really only used on normal roads, or because they believe the bull bar will give them extra protection in an accident. In fact a bull bar probably won't improve your chances in an accident with another vehicle, and it might confuse your airbag sensor and cause the airbag to inflate at the wrong moment. Heavy and rigidly mounted bull bars can injure pedestrians, motorcyclists and cyclists. Other road users can also find bull bars unnecessarily intimidating. If you are thinking of fitting a bull bar, or if your vehicle already has one, ask yourself whether it is really very sensible.

research

Information about safety and environmental research can be found on the website.

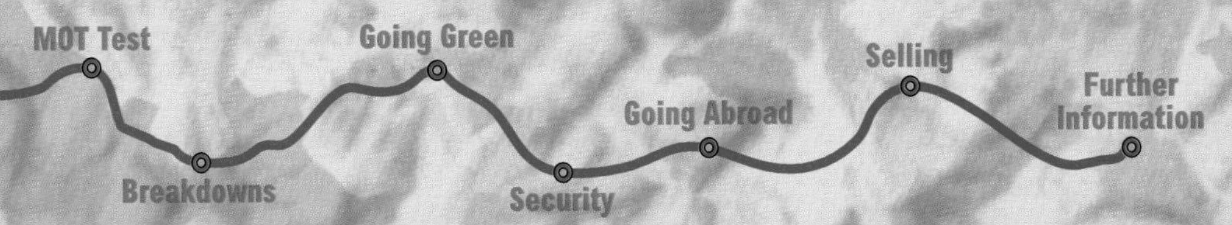

chapter four

# insurance

legal requirements

types of cover

pass plus

frequently asked questions

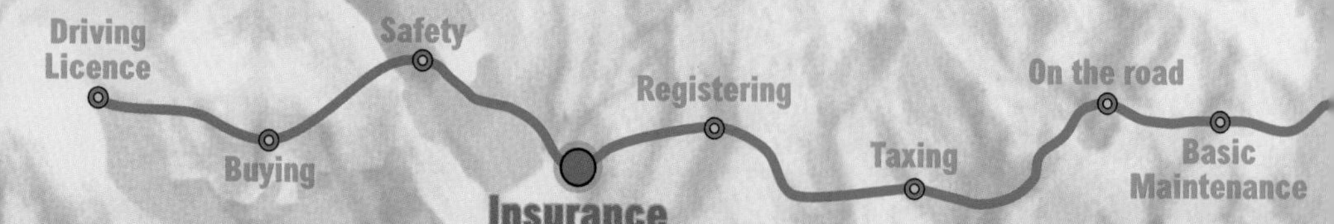

## Insurance – legal requirements



Driving without insurance cover is irresponsible and illegal. If you cause injury to anyone or damage to property, it could be expensive and could result in prosecution. Before taking a vehicle on the road, arrange proper cover with either an insurance company, a broker, the manufacturer or dealer.

- it is illegal to drive without motor insurance
- do not buy a car you can not afford to insure
- if driving someone else's vehicle, check that you are insured.

## Types of cover

**Third party** – is the legal minimum and the cheapest. A third party is anyone you may injure or whose property you may damage. This cover does not protect you for damage to your own vehicle or injury to yourself.

**Third party fire and theft** – in addition to third party cover (above) it also covers you against theft or damage by fire.

**Comprehensive** – This is the best, but most expensive type of insurance. Apart from covering other persons and property from injury and damage, it also covers

- damage to your vehicle
- personal injury to yourself



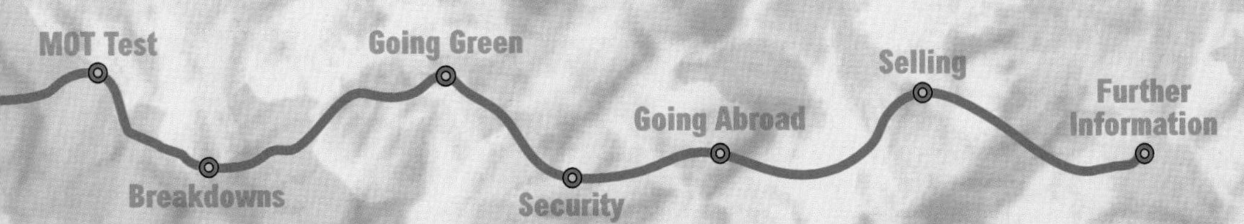

## Pass Plus

The Pass Plus scheme is backed by the government, Driving Standards Agency (DSA) and insurers. It is designed to make newly qualified drivers become better drivers and gives you a number of other benefits, such as cheaper motor insurance.

The course consists of six specially designed training sessions to follow on from a successful driving test – driving in town, out of town, in all weathers, at night, on dual carriageways and on motorways.

The extra experience and positive driving skills gained from Pass Plus would otherwise take a long time to acquire. You should be a safer and better driver. Remember, new drivers make up just 10 per cent of licence holders, but are involved in 19 per cent of accidents.

You can take Pass Plus up to a year after passing your practical driving test. There is no further test to take. When your instructor is satisfied with your performance you receive a certificate from DSA.

Motor insurers that support the scheme may give you one year's no-claims bonus for comprehensive, third party fire and theft and third party policies as soon as you insure your own car. The saving could more than cover the cost of the extra lessons.

You can defer the no-claims bonus for two years if you currently drive under someone else's policy. This means that if you buy a car within two years of completing a Pass Plus course and have not had any claims in the meantime, your first premium may be reduced by the extra one year's no-claims bonus.

The following insurers have agreed to give discounts:

Admiral
CGU (General Accident/Commercial Union)
Churchill
Co-operative Insurance
Cornish Mutual
Diamond
Direct Line
Eagle Star
Ecclesiastical



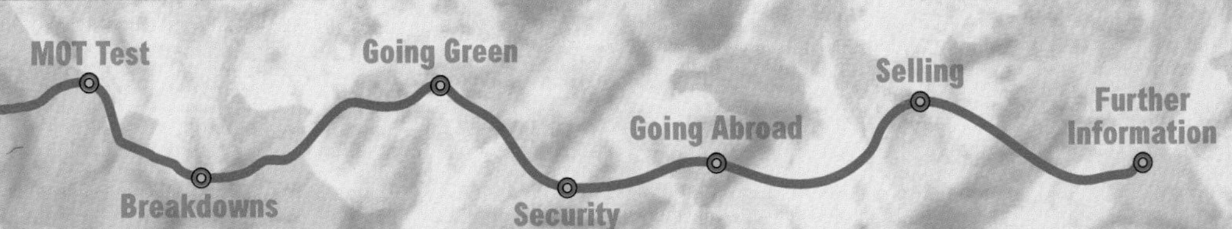

Highway Motor Policies at Lloyds
Norwich Union
Pearl
Privilege
Provident Insurance plc
Royal and SunAlliance
Zurich

Information is correct at time of going to press.

For further information telephone Driving Standards Agency Pass Plus information: 0115 901 2633
or check out the website.

## Frequently asked questions

### How much will it cost?

Shop around for the best deal. It is sensible to do this before you decide on a make of vehicle. The cost will vary from company to company and will depend on

- what cover you want
- how old you are
- how long you've been driving
- where you live and your type of vehicle.

### What will I need to tell the insurers?

Contracts of insurance are contracts of the utmost good faith. You must tell the insurer everything that is relevant. This will include the make and model of your vehicle, the date you passed your test, the intended use and any motoring convictions.

### What is insured?

This varies from policy to policy. Read the small print. If you make a claim for damage to your vehicle, you may have to pay the first £50 or £100 yourself. This is called the excess.

### What is the Certificate?

A short and simple document detailing the conditions – including who is insured, the type of cover and vehicle and the expiry date.

### Will I need to show my Certificate to anyone?

Yes. You will need to show it at the post office when you renew your vehicle excise licence (tax disc). You may also be asked to produce it if you are stopped by the police or involved in an accident.

### What should I do if I am involved in an accident?

If you are in collision with another vehicle and any person or large animal is injured, or damage is caused to any other vehicle or property, you must stop and give your name and address to anyone having reasonable cause to require them.

### What details should I give?

Your name and (if different) the vehicle owner's name and address, the name of your insurers and the vehicle's registration number.

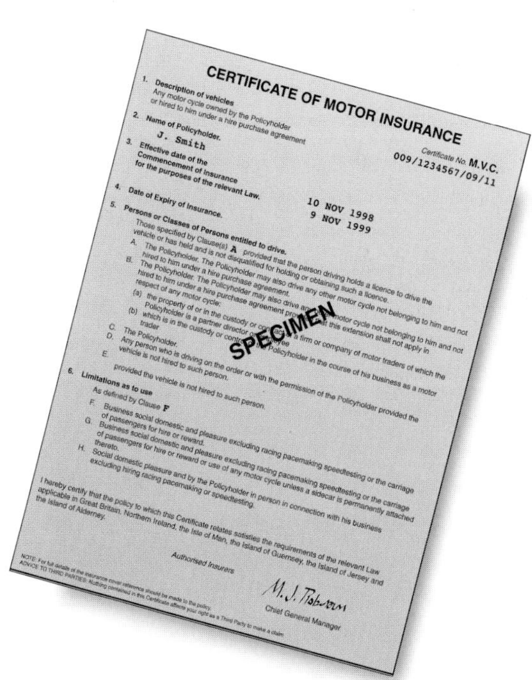

CERTIFICATE OF MOTOR INSURANCE

Certificate No. M.V.C. 009/1234567/09/11

1. **Description of vehicles**
   Any motor cycle owned by the Policyholder or hired to him under a hire purchase agreement
2. **Name of Policyholder.**
   J. Smith
3. **Effective date of the Commencement of Insurance for the purposes of the relevant Law.** 10 NOV 1998
4. **Date of Expiry of Insurance.** 9 NOV 1999
5. **Persons or Classes of Persons entitled to drive.**
   Those specified by Clause(s) **A** provided that the person driving holds a licence to drive the vehicle or has held and is not disqualified for holding or obtaining such a licence.
   A. The Policyholder. The Policyholder may also drive any other motor cycle not belonging to him and not hired to him under a hire purchase agreement.
   B. The Policyholder. The Policyholder may also drive an[illegible] motor cycle not belonging to him and not hired to him under a hire purchase agreement prov[illegible]at this extension shall not apply in respect of any motor cycle:
   (a) the property of or in the custody or con[illegible] a firm or company of motor traders of which the Policyholder is a partner director o[illegible]ployee
   (b) which is in the custody or control [illegible] Policyholder in the course of his business as a motor trader
   C. The Policyholder.
   D. Any person who is driving on the order or with the permission of the Policyholder provided the vehicle is not hired to such person.
   E. provided the vehicle is not hired to such person.
6. **Limitations as to use**
   As defined by Clause **F**
   F. Business social domestic and pleasure excluding racing pacemaking speedtesting or the carriage of passengers for hire or reward.
   G. Business social domestic and pleasure excluding racing pacemaking speedtesting or the carriage of passengers for hire or reward or use of any motor cycle unless a sidecar is permanently attached thereto.
   H. Social domestic pleasure and by the Policyholder in person in connection with his business excluding hiring racing pacemaking or speedtesting.

I hereby certify that the policy to which this Certificate relates satisfies the requirements of the relevant Law applicable in Great Britain, Northern Ireland, the Isle of Man, the Island of Guernsey, the Island of Jersey and the Island of Alderney.

Authorised Insurers

M. J. Robson

Chief General Manager

SPECIMEN

NOTE: For full details of the insurance cover reference should be made to the policy.
ADVICE TO THIRD PARTIES: Nothing contained in this Certificate affects your right as a Third Party to make a claim.



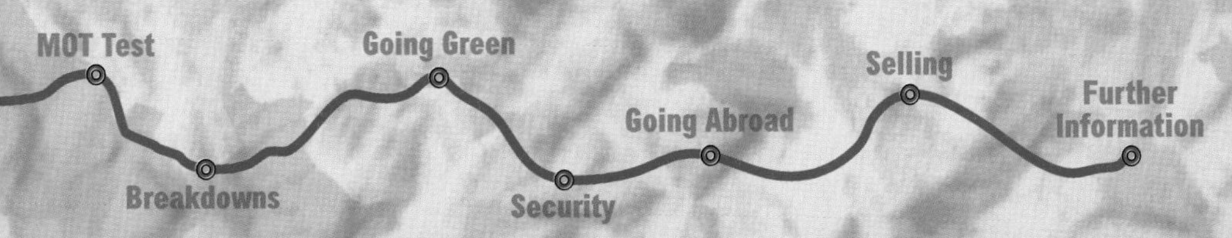

chapter five

# registering your car

documentation

importing a vehicle

registration numbers

personalised registrations

frequently asked questions

## Documentation

history

Every vehicle must be registered as part of keeping it on or off the road. This involves giving the vehicle a unique identification, i.e. a registration mark (number plates), and giving DVLA details of the vehicle itself and the keeper. The Registration Document proves that this has been done. A Registration Document shows the registered keeper of the vehicle, that is, the person who keeps the vehicle on a public road, not necessarily the legal owner. It gives the keeper's name and address, the registration mark and other information about the vehicle. A new Registration Document is issued each time DVLA updates the record with any change to the existing details.

Registration Document

DVLA now issues a new style three-part Registration Document, in three colours:

| | |
|---|---|
| • V5 (blue) | Keeper Details |
| • V5/2 (green) | New Keeper Supplement |
| • V5/3 (red) | Notification of Sale/Transfer to the Motor Trade |

The new document requires both buyer and seller to notify a change of keeper on the same form. The keeper selling the vehicle has a legal responsibility for completing the V5. Explanatory notes are on the back of the document; always refer to these before notifying DVLA of any change.

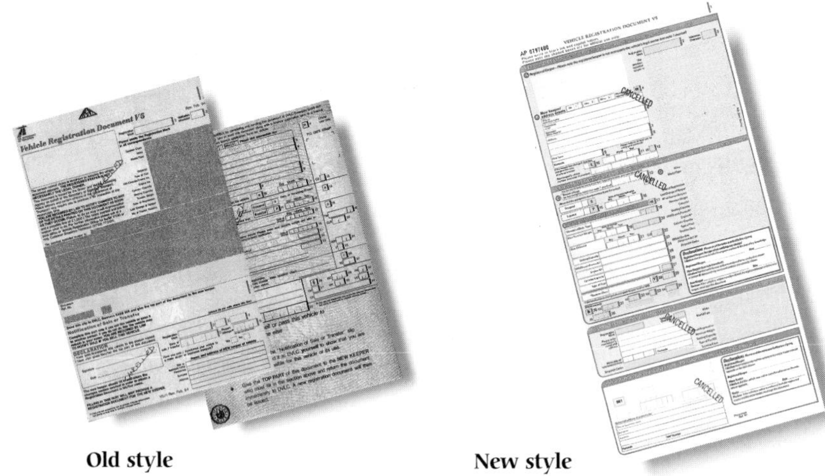

Old style

New style

Registration Document

## New style and old style registration documents

Unless the vehicle is registered in your name you will not be sent a renewal reminder form when the vehicle excise licence (road tax) expires. Also, it may not be possible for the manufacturer to contact you if there is a potential defect in the vehicle.

Remember, the Registration Document does not prove legal ownership. Before buying a vehicle you should satisfy yourself that the seller either owns the vehicle, or is entitled to offer it for sale. Ask to see the bill of sale in the seller's name or other evidence such as a hire purchase discharge document.

If you are buying privately, you should view the vehicle at the address shown on the Registration Document.



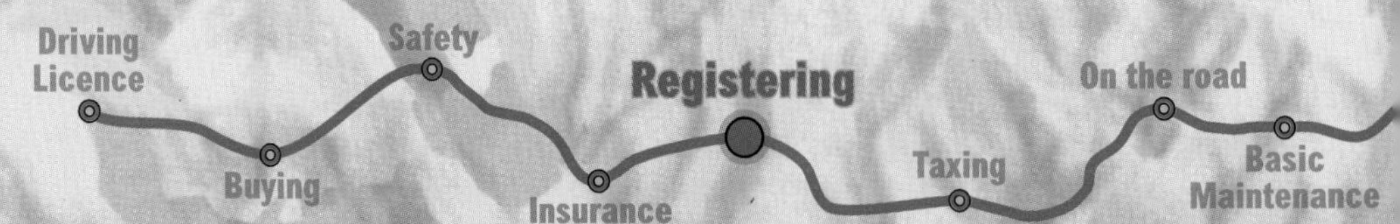

You should also check that the vehicle identification number (VIN) printed on the Registration Document corresponds with the VIN on the vehicle itself (usually to be found on a metal plate in the engine compartment).

If the vehicle is not registered in the seller's name, or a Registration Document is not available, ask why. If you are in any serious doubt about the ownership of the vehicle do not proceed with the purchase.

You should keep your registration documents in a safe place. Do not keep them in the car.

## First registration fee

first fee

A fee of £25 is payable on the first registration and licensing of a motor vehicle in the United Kingdom. The fee is designed to cover the administration costs associated with registration of the vehicle throughout its life. The fee is applicable to all vehicles except those first registered and licensed in the 'disabled exempt' taxation class.

Registering vehicles, and keeping the register up to date when keepers move and vehicles change hands are important weapons in the fight against vehicle related and other crime. The initial registration fee insures that more of the cost of this service is placed on those who call upon it.

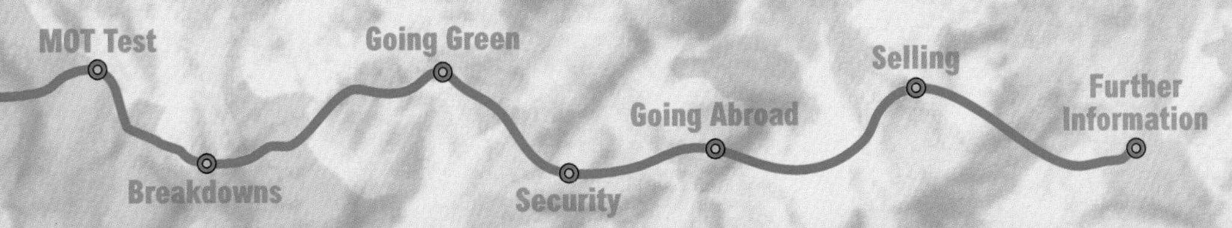

## Importing a vehicle

A vehicle permanently imported into Great Britain must be registered immediately with DVLA. After arrival it may be driven on foreign registration plates only from the port of entry to your home address or to a pre-arranged mechanical test. Thereafter, it must be kept off-road until the licensing and registration formalities have been completed.

Local Offices

Registration takes place at one of DVLA's 40 Local Offices. A list of offices is in chapter 15.

You will need to produce the following:

Registration Document

- the duty payable
- completed form V55/5
- £25 registration fee
- Insurance Certificate
- a receipted invoice from supplier
- evidence of type approval
- Customs and Excise form
- MOT Certificate (if appropriate)
- foreign documents relating to the vehicle.

To be classified as 'new' an imported vehicle must

- be registered within 14 days of collection or first use abroad
- only have accrued reasonable delivery mileage
- not have been previously registered permanently abroad.



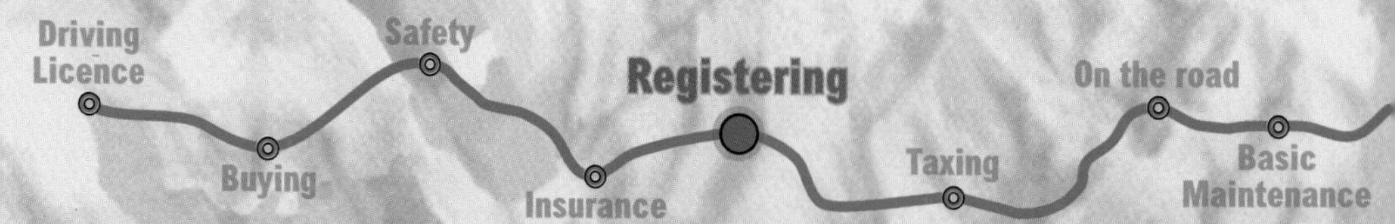

### HM Customs and Excise

VAT is payable on imported vehicles. You must tell Customs and Excise within seven days of importing a vehicle. If you personally acquire a new vehicle from another EU member state, DVLA will notify Customs and Excise on your behalf. In order to do so you will be required to complete a VAT415, available from a DVLA Local Office. If you do not intend to use or keep the vehicle on the road, you do not have to register it, but you will still need to notify Customs.

## Registration numbers

The age identification letter on vehicle registration plates now changes every six months, in March and September. The change was designed to smooth out the August sales peak. The current format of registration numbers will continue until the prefix series is exhausted at the end of August 2001. After the 'Y' series the registration period will be shown as a two digit number. The second of these numbers will match the year in which the car was first registered.

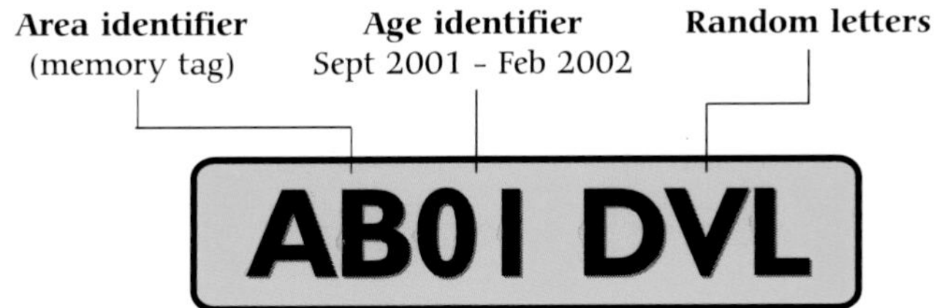

Registration numbers must be correctly displayed in accordance with the regulations governing the design, manufacture and display of vehicle registration number plates. It is an offence to mis-space or mis-represent registrations or number plates or to use fixing bolts to obliterate or enhance any of the characters to corrupt numbers to appear as letters or vice versa. There is a maximum fine of up to £1,000 and vehicles with illegally displayed number plates will fail the MOT test. You should also be aware that in some cases the registration number may be withdrawn permanently from use.

## Personalised registrations

cherished numbers

You may elect to buy and assign a personalised registration either through DVLA or through a cherished number dealer.

DVLA has a sales scheme offering a unique range of distinctive and individual registrations, all of which have never previously been issued.

DVLA's service is available through its dedicated Select Registrations Hotline or through one of its Classic Collection and Custom Marks auctions.



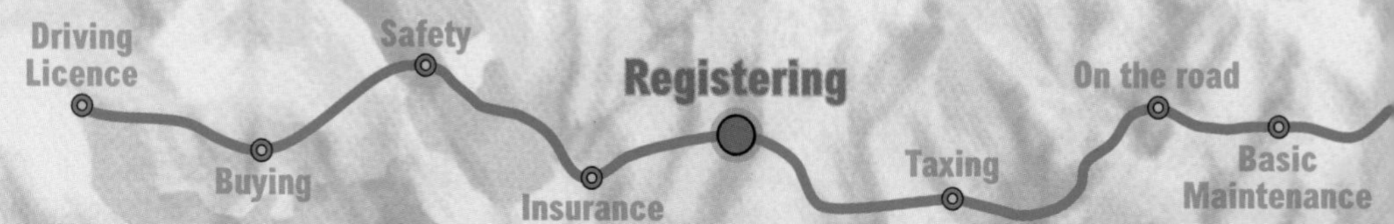

## Frequently asked questions



### When should I register and license an imported vehicle?

You must register and license the vehicle before it is used or kept on a public road. Remember that to be classified as 'new' a vehicle must be registered within 14 days of collection or first use abroad.

### Do I have to tell Customs?

It is a legal requirement to notify HM Customs within seven days of arrival in Great Britain. If you are registering the vehicle within seven days of arrival, DVLA will notify Customs on your behalf (see above under HM Customs and Excise).

### How long can I use the vehicle on foreign plates?

Only *en route* from the port of entry to your home address or other destination or to a pre-arranged test.

### What is a 'new means of transport'?

This is a Customs and Excise term for a vehicle that originates from the EU and is less than six months old or has travelled less than 6,000 kms.



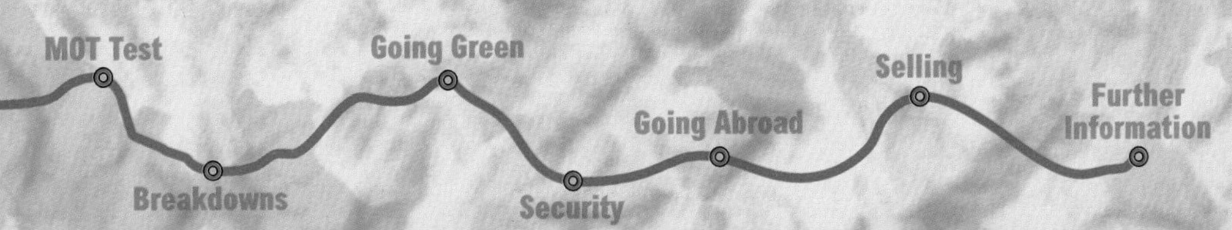

customs forms

## What Customs form do I need to register my vehicle?

This will depend on whether or not you are VAT registered, when you register and where you obtained the vehicle.

Local Offices

- Individuals who have personally acquired a new vehicle from another member state – VAT 415 (available from DVLA local offices)
- Individuals registering a new vehicle acquired from another member state direct to Customs – VAT 413
- Individuals registering a personal import [any age vehicle] from outside the EU – C&E 386
- Individuals registering a 'restricted' personal import [any age vehicle] from outside the EU – C&E 388
- VAT registered traders acquiring commercially within the EU – VAT 414
- VAT registered traders commercially importing vehicles from outside the EU – C&E 389.

## I am a British Serviceman/woman. Do I use the same forms?

No. You must use BFG 414 which is the form issued to all customs-relieved vehicles personally acquired within the European Union by British Forces Germany (BFG) personnel.

## What are DVLA Select Registrations and how do I buy?

Select Registrations

Select Registrations are made up of certain prefixed period identifiers followed by a series of numbers followed by a



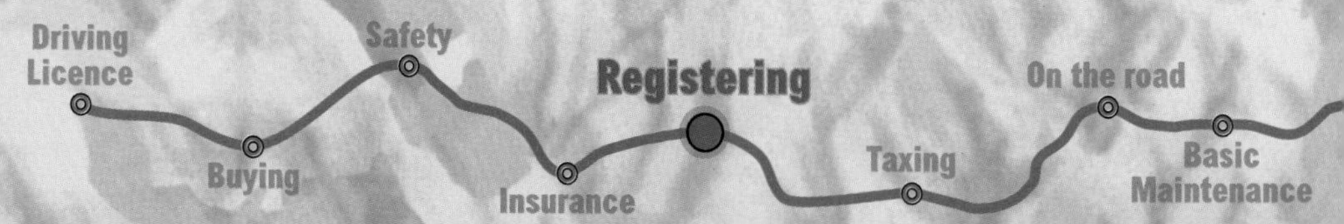

combination of three letters. They are priced at a couple of hundred pounds including VAT plus an Assignment Fee.

If you want to see what your preferred number looks like or check whether it is available, visit the website which lists all available Select Registrations along with the price. When you are ready to buy, call DVLA's Registration Hotline on 0870 6000 142 – they are open Monday to Friday between 9.00am and 5.00pm and you can pay by cheque, or Mastercard/Visa. The Registration Hotline will also advise on the availability of your preferred registration number.

## What are Custom Marks and how do I buy?

Custom Marks

DVLA Custom Marks are of personal and of specific interest to individuals or organisations. DVLA Custom Marks auctions are held every four to six months in Bristol.

## What is DVLA's Classic Collection and how do I buy?

Classic Collection

DVLA's Classic Collection is exclusive and attractive, with universal appeal. They are offered for sale at prestigious venues around the country.

## Where can I find out more about DVLA's auctions?

DVLA's auctions are advertised in the national and appropriate regional press and described on the DVLA website. Here you can see the full list of registrations that make up the next auction and find useful information about the process.

If you want to be added to DVLA's auction mailing list, write to DVLA Sale of Marks (Marketing), Swansea SA99 1DN with details of your preferred registration if you have one.

## What should I consider before I buy?

Whether you buy through our telesales business or at auction you need to think about several things:

- if the number contains a year letter either at the front or the end of the number, make sure that your vehicle is the right age to receive it. Remember you cannot make a vehicle appear younger than it actually is
- your vehicle must be registered at an address in England, Scotland or Wales to be able to get the number put on your vehicle
- be satisfied that the number you intend buying is the one you are being sold. Once bought, there is no turning back
- don't buy if you intend misrepresenting your number, that is, spacing it incorrectly.

## Can I transfer my number to another vehicle?

transfers

The Cherished Transfer Scheme enables an assigned registration number to be moved directly from one vehicle to another. Only the registered keeper of a vehicle is entitled to apply to transfer its number. Application form V317 (Transfer of Registration Mark) must be completed and a transfer fee of £80 paid. If the vehicle receiving the number in a cherished transfer is already registered, its existing number will become void unless an application to transfer or retain that number is made at the same time. To be eligible to participate in the cherished transfer scheme, vehicles must be registered at DVLA, currently licensed, of a type that is subject to an annual roadworthiness test, and available for inspection. The V317 application form explains the rules in more detail.

## I have sold my car but want to keep the number; what do I do?

retention

The Retention Scheme enables a number to be held apart from the vehicle it has been assigned to, for a 12-month period pending its reassignment to another vehicle. Only the registered keeper of a vehicle is entitled to apply for a right of retention.

Application form V778/1 (Retention of Vehicle Registration Mark) must be completed and the application fee is £25 plus an assignment fee of £80, bringing the total payable to



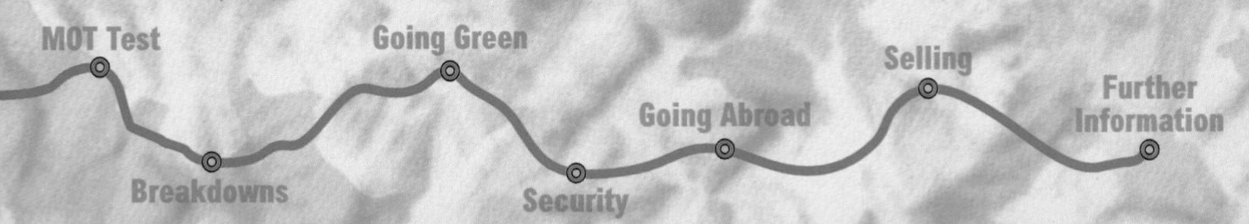

retention

£105. To be eligible to participate in the retention scheme, the vehicle must be registered at DVLA, currently licensed, of a type that is subject to an annual roadworthiness test, and available for inspection. The V778/1 application form explains the rules in more detail.

Successful applicants are issued with a V778 Retention Document, valid for 12 months, which records details of the registration number, the grantee (the applicant), and nominee details where supplied in the application. If, after you have received your document, you wish to add or change nominee details, you will need to reapply with a fee of £25.

If before the end of the 12-month period you decide that you would like to extend entitlement for a further 12-month period you can simply use the Retention Document to apply together with the fee of £25.

These prices apply at the time of printing, check out the website for up to date costs.



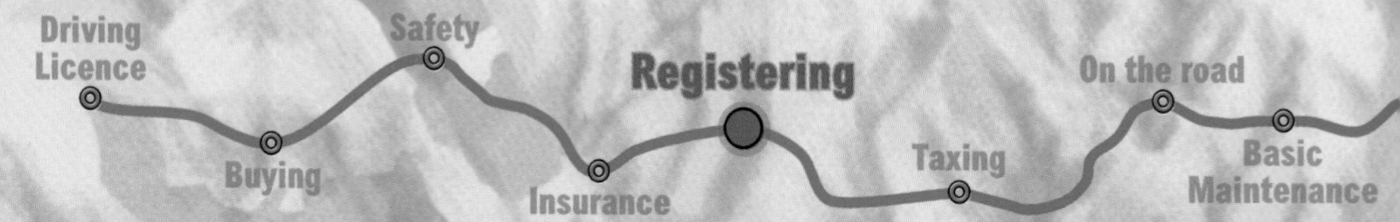

## Where else can I obtain a registration number?

If you are interested in having a registration number which is already in circulation you will find private and trade advertisements in the National Press or Specialist Magazines. Dealers in personalised numbers may offer for sale assigned numbers which are from their 'stock' or may act as agent for the motorist who wishes to sell the number of his or her vehicle. In either case, the movement of the number from one vehicle to another can only be achieved through DVLA's Cherished Transfer or Retention facilities. Dealers may also act for you in obtaining a previously unissued number from DVLA Sales Scheme, but you can expect to pay them for their services.

RMIF

The Cherished Number Dealers Association is a trade association of certain registration number dealers affiliated to the Retail Motor Industry Federation. The Association has set standards of trading which include providing written terms and conditions of business for their customers.

CNDA

Members of the Association can be identified by the CNDA logo on their advertisements. If you would like more information about the services offered by the CNDA or a list of its members you can write to the Director, CNDA, 2nd Floor, Chestnut House, 32 North Street, Rugby, CV21 2AH or telephone the helpline on 01788 538302.

## What if I have a special number on my vehicle and I want to rebuild the vehicle or convert it to a kit?

Not all registration numbers are transferable. Check your Registration Document first. If it is transferable, you should secure it before carrying out any alterations/conversions, in case entitlement to the number is lost.

## What if my vehicle is stolen and not recovered?

If your vehicle is stolen and has not been recovered after a year, you can apply to have its registration number transferred to your replacement vehicle, providing certain conditions are met. In order to qualify for the concession, the theft must have been notified to the police and recorded at DVLA as stolen for not less than 12 months. In addition, at the time of the theft the vehicle must have had a current vehicle excise licence (tax disc). The DVLA will also require a letter from your insurers confirming that they have no objection to the number being reissued. This must be provided because once insurers have settled your claim, they have a rightful claim to the vehicle should it be recovered.

To apply, or for further information, write quoting the registration number to Cherished Transfer Section, D11, DVLA, Swansea SA6 7JL. If you wish to telephone, DVLA's Customer Enquiries number is 0870 240 0010.



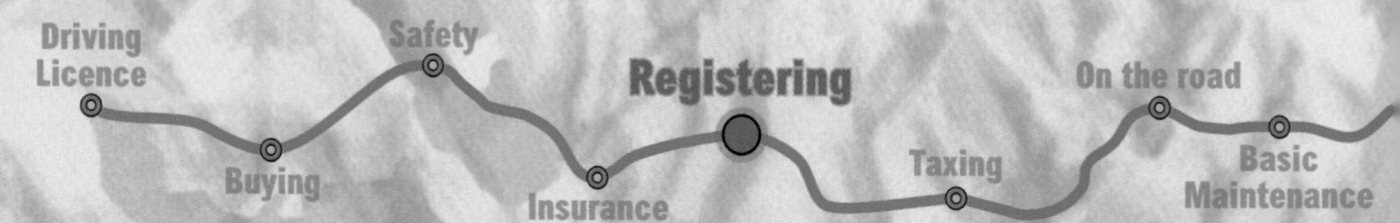

## What if my vehicle is 'written off'?

A vehicle is 'written off' when it is judged by insurers to be beyond economical repair. In such a case, the insurance company agrees a pay-out with the insured, and legal ownership of the vehicle then passes to the insurance company. The company is then free to sell the vehicle as salvage and the purchaser may repair it and put it back on the road.

If your vehicle is written off, you may still apply to transfer or retain its number providing

- your insurers have not disposed of the vehicle and
- the vehicle is available for inspection and
- you can satisfy all the conditions of the transfer or retention schemes.

**IMPORTANT**: It essential that you discuss your personalised registration number with your insurers at the outset. You will need to ensure they are aware that in the event of a write-off, the vehicle must be made available for inspection by DVLA if you are to transfer or retain the number. If your insurers settle your claim and sell the vehicle as salvage before the number is properly transferred or retained, the mark will pass with the vehicle to the new keeper and you will lose your entitlement. You will also lose entitlement if the vehicle is sent for scrapping before the number is transferred or retained.



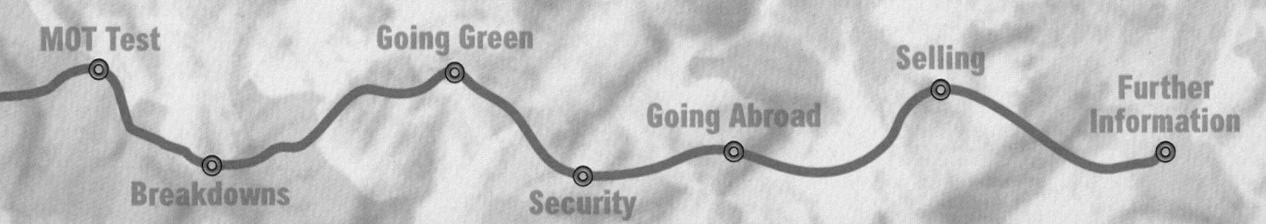

Once you have successfully transferred or retained your registration number from the written off vehicle, let your insurers know about the change of number and send them the amended V5 Registration Document. If your insurers intend to sell the write-off as salvage, the vehicle must display the replacement registration number.

### What if my vehicle has been scrapped?

Scrapping occurs when a vehicle, whether an insurance write-off or not, is broken up for spares or otherwise destroyed. Once a vehicle ceases to exist its registration number is cancelled. If your vehicle has been scrapped, you will not be able to transfer its registration number.

The law requires the person who actually breaks up or destroys the vehicle to notify DVLA that the vehicle has been scrapped and return the V5 Registration Document.

DVLA

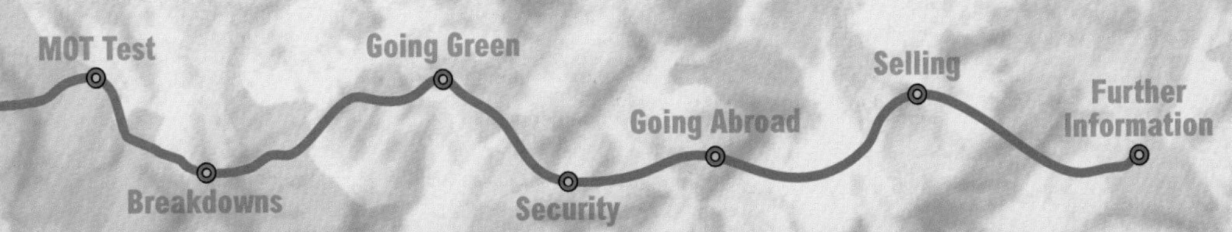
MOT Test
Breakdowns
Going Green
Security
Going Abroad
Selling
Further Information

## chapter six

# taxing your car

vehicle excise duty

statutory off-road notification (SORN)

historic vehicles

trying to get away with it

frequently asked questions

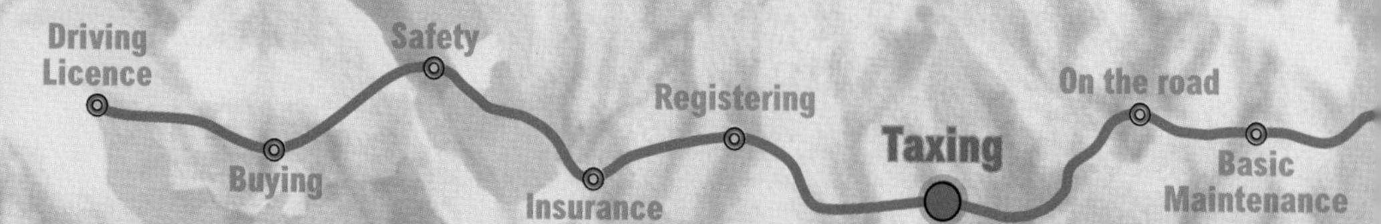

## Vehicle excise duty

VED bands

A Vehicle Excise Licence is is normally referred to as a tax disc. The disc, which must be displayed on the left-hand side on your car windsceen, shows that the excise duty has been paid. You can buy your licence to last six or twelve months.

emissions

If you bought a new car after 1 March 2001 the Vehicle Excise Duty (VED) will be based on the vehicle's carbon dioxide ($CO_2$) emission figure and the type of fuel it uses (see table below). A low $CO_2$ output means greater efficiency, so you won't just be doing your bit for the environment, you'll also make substantial savings in tax and running costs. A four-band system applies to each type of fuel.

how much?

| | A | B | D | E |
|---|---|---|---|---|
| $CO_2$ emission figure (g/km)* | Up to 150 | 151 to 165 | 166 to 185 | over 185 |
| 1 Alternative fuel car | £90 | £110 | £130 | £150 |
| 2 Petrol car | £100 | £120 | £140 | £155 |
| 3 Diesel car | £110 | £130 | £150 | £160 |

* g/km = grammes of $CO_2$ per kilometre travelled

## Statutory off road notification (SORN)

A vehicle driven, parked or even left unused on a public road must be licensed. If it is not, you may be fined as well as having to pay an additional penalty. There are two separate offences: not displaying a current licence, and using or keeping a vehicle on the public road without a current vehicle licence.

### There is one exception

An unlicensed vehicle, provided it is insured, may be driven direct to and from a testing station for a pre-arranged compulsory test. If your licence has just expired you may continue to use the vehicle for up to 14 days after its expiry. But within that period you must have applied for a new one, to run from the day after the last one expired. Please note that this 14-day period of grace is a concession. In law a current licence must be displayed at all times when the vehicle is on the road.

### Declaring SORN

If the keeper of a vehicle does not license the vehicle because it is not used or kept on a public road, DVLA must be told as soon as the vehicle is taken off the road. The requirement to make a declaration only applies to vehicles for which a licence was in force on or after 31 January 1998.



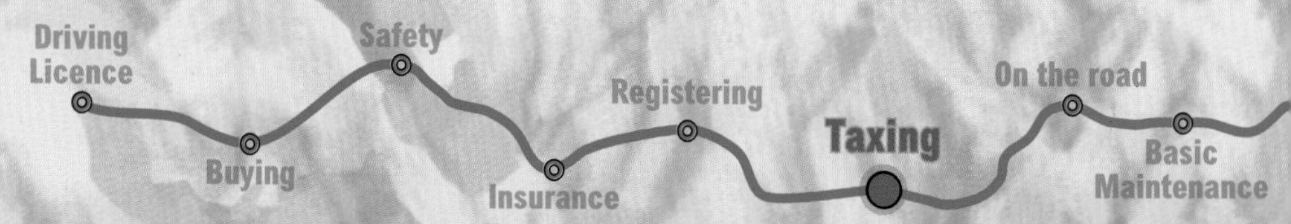

If you do not license the vehicle because you have taken it off the road (for repair for example) you must declare SORN immediately instead. You may use your vehicle licence renewal reminder V11 or V85/1 to do this. The V11 is designed for use at the Post Office, while the V85/1 is for use at the DVLA Local Office. Do not send either to DVLA, Swansea.

You must also declare SORN if you take the vehicle off the road and claim a refund of duty on your licence, but only if the vehicle remains in your possession. Please do not notify SORN if the vehicle has been sold, scrapped, stolen or exported. If you need to declare SORN and you do not have a V11 or a V85/1 and are not applying for a refund of duty, you can use form V890. This form is available from the DVLA Customer Enquiries Unit or from your nearest DVLA Local Office.

V890 download

Local Offices

## Historic vehicles

If your vehicle was constructed before 1 January 1973 you may be eligible to license your vehicle in the Historic Vehicle taxation class. Vehicles licensed in the exempt Historic class are not subject to Vehicle Excise Duty but must still display a vehicle licence disc (tax disc) and be licensed annually.

## Licensing a vehicle in the Historic Vehicle taxation class

Local Offices

The first time you license a vehicle in this class you must apply to a DVLA Local Office. You need to take with you:

- the Vehicle Registration Document (V5). This must clearly show a date of registration or manufacture of the vehicle prior to 1 January 1973*. If the Registration Document is not available or if you think the age shown is incorrect, you will need to produce a dating certificate from a vehicle enthusiasts' club or evidence from the vehicle manufacturer

*Note: Where a registration document indicates that the vehicle was registered up to and including 7 January 1973, DVLA are prepared to allow entry into the Historic Class on the basis that the vehicle would have been constructed the previous year

- an appropriate test certificate (if applicable)
- a valid certificate of insurance
- completed licence application form V10 – available from any Post Office or from a DVLA Local Office.



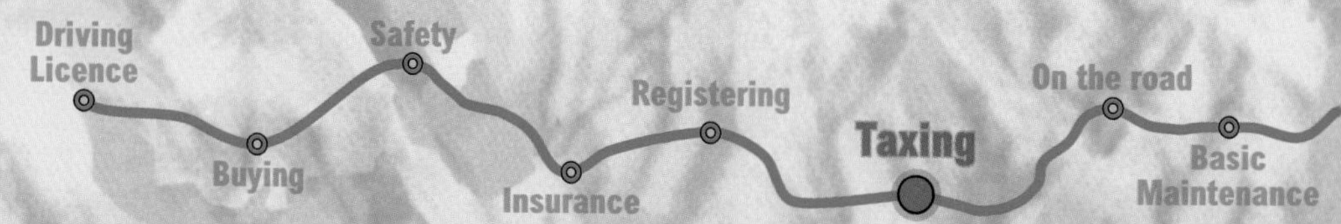

## Trying to get away with it

Local Offices

Enforcement action, including prosecution, is taken against any vehicle keeper who uses or keeps an unlicenced vehicle on the public road. In addition, powers now exist for such vehicles to be wheel clamped and impounded.

A public road includes lay-bys, grass verges, pavements and parking bays etc that are maintained at public expense. DVLA gives authority to its appointed wheel clamping contractor to operate the wheel clamping scheme. The scheme applies to all vehicle types.

### If your vehicle is clamped

If your vehicle is clamped for tax evasion, you will find an information card on your windscreen telling you what to do. To have the clamp removed from your vehicle you must either

clamping

- pay a declamping fee of £68 and purchase a valid tax disc, which must be taken in person to the vehicle pound identified on the information card for it to be examined

  or

- pay a declamping fee of £68 and pay an additional surety fee of £100. The surety is refundable on sight of a valid tax disc within 14 days.

If at the time of clamping, you had a valid tax disc but it was not displayed on your vehicle you may be able to get your vehicle declamped for free. To be eligible you must telephone the vehicle pound straight away and give them full details of the tax disc. The tax disc must be taken in person to the pound immediately to be examined. If all requirements are met, no fees will be charged.

If you do not claim your vehicle within 24 hours, it will be removed to a secure vehicle pound. Higher release charges and daily storage charges will apply.

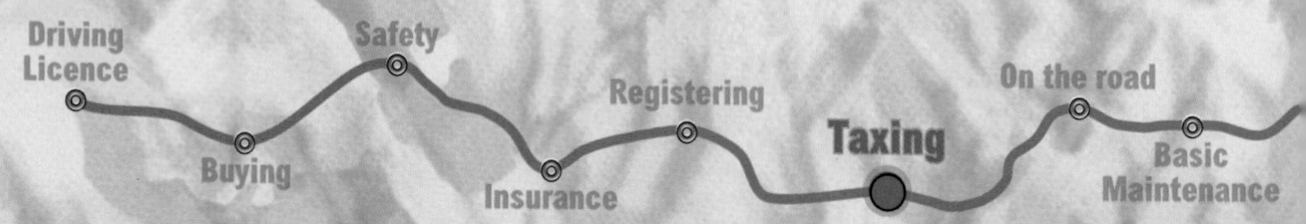

## Frequently asked questions

### What if my car was first registered before 1 March 2001?

It will continue to be taxed according to engine size.

### How do I know what band my car falls into?

VED bands

Check out the website where there is a database showing you the details. There is also a booklet entitled 'New Fuel Consumption and Emission Figures' available at most motor dealers.

### I am planning to change my car. Can I transfer the tax disc to the new one?

V14 download

No, but you can apply for a refund, providing you have at least one complete calendar month still to run. You need to fill in form V14 and send it with the licence to: Refund Section, DVLA, Swansea, SA99 1AL.

It must be received before the first day of the month. (Proof of posting is advisable). Alternatively you can present it at one of DVLA's Local Offices.

Local Offices



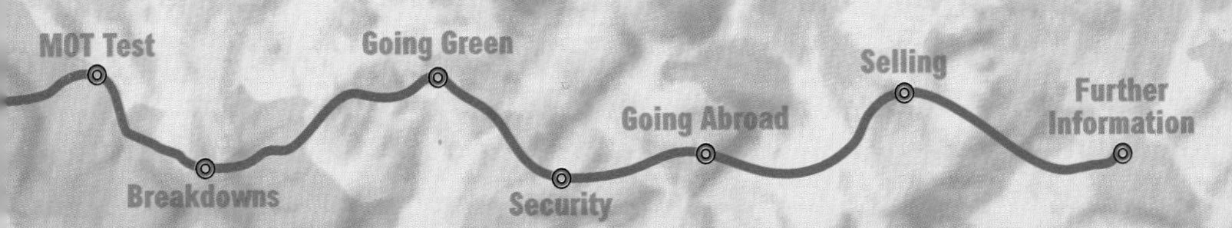

new vehicle

## How do I licence a new vehicle?

When you buy a new vehicle the dealer will usually apply on your behalf for the first vehicle licence at the same time as applying for the Registration Document. The vehicle should therefore be licensed when you take delivery. If the dealer does not apply for you, make sure that the dealer gives you the application form (V55) so that you can apply to a DVLA Local Office yourself.

In either case make sure that your full name, address and postcode and other details on the form are stated clearly and correctly, as these details will be used to set up the vehicle record and will appear on the Registration Document.

Local Offices

## I bought a used car without a tax disc, how do I apply for one?

You need to apply for your tax disc on form V10. You can get one of these at Post Offices or DVLA Local Offices.

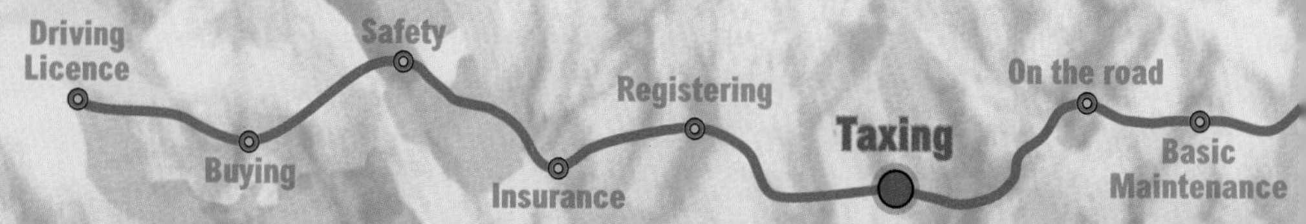

## Will DVLA remind me when I need to renew my tax disc?

About a fortnight before your vehicle licence expires, DVLA will send a renewal application form V11 to the address shown on the Registration Document. You should therefore ensure that DVLA has your current address. You can use this form to relicense the vehicle provided that the date from which the licence is to run, the vehicle details and taxation class printed on the form are still correct.

SORN

You do not need to show your Registration Document unless you have changed your name or address. If you have received form V11 and will not be using or keeping the vehicle on a public road, you can use the form to declare statutory off-road notification (SORN), as mentioned previously.

If you do not receive a renewal form for any reason this is no defence for not relicensing your vehicle. You can apply for renewal on form V10.

## When can I apply for a vehicle licence (tax disc)?

Not more than 14 days before the licence is to start. But if there has been a break in licensing of a month or more you cannot be issued with a licence more than two working days before it is due to start. A licence normally comes into force on the day of issue, but if taken out in advance it comes into force on the first day of the following month.

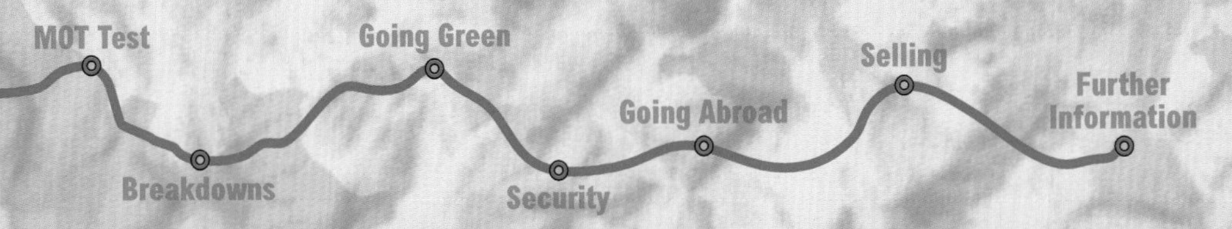

## I cannot get to the Post Office in person. Can I send my application by post?

Yes, you will find a list of postal addresses in chapter 15. You should address the envelope 'Post Office' (MVL Duty).

## What other documents do I need?

You will need to produce:

- the duty payable
- a completed application form
- a valid certificate of insurance
- a vehicle test certificate (MOT) if your vehicle is over three years old.

## I have lost the tax disc for my car. What do I do?

If your vehicle licence is lost, stolen, destroyed, mutilated or accidentally defaced, you must apply for a duplicate using form V20 which is available from licensing Post Offices and DVLA Local Offices. Your application, together with the Registration Document and the fee, should be taken or sent to a DVLA Local Office. Provided the vehicle is currently licensed in your name, you will receive a duplicate covering the full licence period.



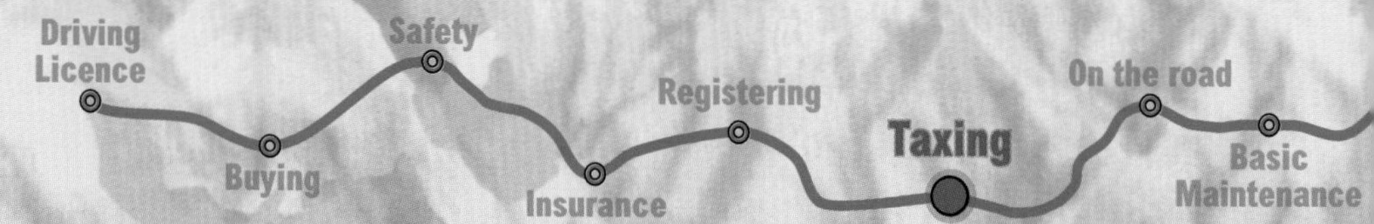

## One of my relations is receiving a disability allowance. Do they have to pay for their licence (tax disc)?

disabled persons

They may be entitled to a free tax disc. The vehicle they drive must be registered in their name and must be used by them or for the purposes of them (for instance, to get shopping or a prescription). In order to apply they will need a Certificate of Entitlement, which is issued by the Benefits Agency. You can get further information from the customer enquiries at DVLA. (see chapter 15) or:

Fylde Benefits Directorate
Disability Living Allowance Unit
Warbreck House
Warbreck Hill
Blackpool
FY2 OYE
Tel: 0345 123456

Advice on War Pensioners Mobility Supplement may be obtained from

War Pensions Agency
Norcross
Blackpool
FY5 3WP
Tel: 01253 858858

disabled persons

**I am a disabled driver. What happens when my vehicle licence disc expires?**

You will receive a vehicle licence reminder form V11, which you must present to the Post Office in the normal way and you will be issued with a new exempt disc.

CLE300/4 download

**My neighbour is running a car without a valid tax disc. Should I report it?**

dvla customer enquiries

Besides the fact your neighbour is breaking the law by not paying road tax, it is possible that there is no insurance or MOT certificate. There is a road safety issue here and taking this car off the road could save lives. Ensuring that DVLA records are kept up to date is crucial when conducting enquiries into traffic offences and vehicle related crime. Reporting your neighbour would therefore assist in road safety and detection of crime involving a vehicle. You should report the vehicle to your DVLA Local Office. You can also download form CLE300/4 (witness statement – reporting an unlicensed vehicle) from the website.



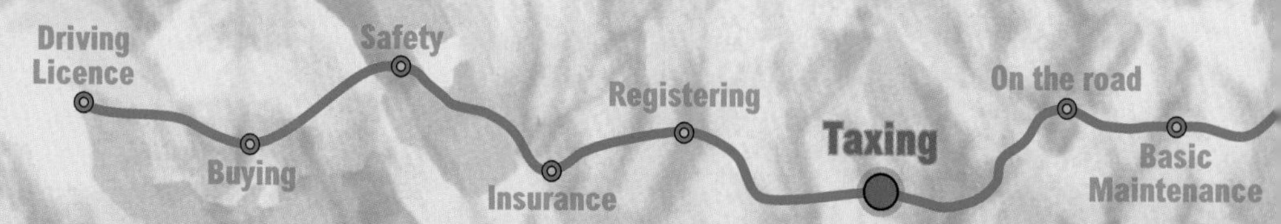

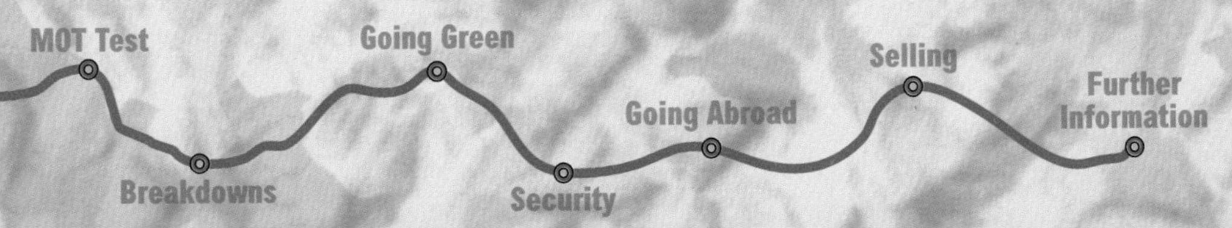
MOT Test
Breakdowns
Going Green
Security
Going Abroad
Selling
Further Information

chapter seven

# on the road

responsibility

towing

passenger safety

child restraints

carrying loads

lights

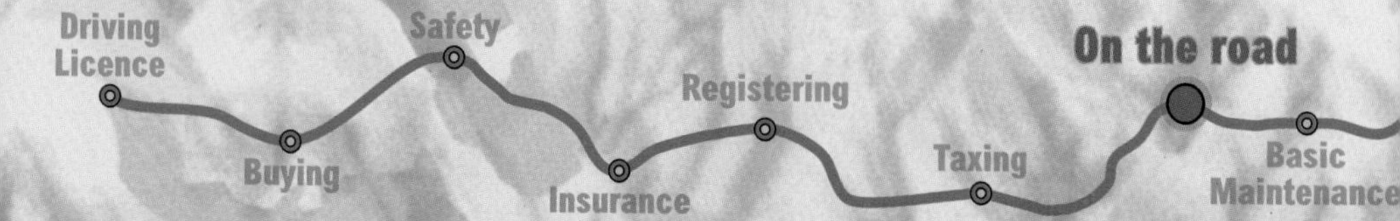

## Responsibility

Owning a car comes with responsibility. Whether you have just passed your test or have been driving for years the same applies. No matter how good, how fast, how expensive or how efficient your vehicle is, it's you, the driver, who determines whether it's a safe means of transport.

Driver skill and driver attitude are two key areas which determine your approach behind the wheel.

There is, after all, a lot of enjoyment and satisfaction to be gained from showing not only your skill and ability but also courtesy and consideration to those around you. Apart from the reward of a nod or smile in appreciation, you'll have the added satisfaction of knowing you are making our roads that much safer. The right attitude and behaviour are the key factors to becoming a good driver.

A good driver isn't a perfect driver; it's very doubtful if such a driver exists. Nevertheless, apart from skill and experience, which only come with time, a good driver needs

- responsibility
- concentration
- anticipation
- patience
- confidence.

safety tips
road safety strategy
think!
traffic news

## health and safety

Together, these qualities go to make up what is generally known as the driver's attitude. It is attitude which, in turn, influences driver behaviour.

Developing the right attitude and behaviour will come easier to some drivers than others, but these attributes are so important to safe driving that it's vital for every driver to make the effort to keep working on them. Take pride in your driving and remember that, even if you have been driving for years, there's always something to learn.

## accident statistics

There are approximately 3,400 fatal accidents every year in the UK. It's a fact that nearly all road accidents are caused, to some degree, by the driver. Reducing them is the responsibility of every driver.

Buying a car with the best safety features (both primary and secondary) can prevent mistakes becoming accidents or reduce the seriousness of an accident (primary safety). It can also reduce the severity of injuries you may suffer if an accident occurs (secondary safety).

## what if?

These accidents usually involve other cars whose drivers are not at fault and who may have had no chance to take avoiding action. Improving your driving skills can reduce the risk of you having an accident – why not consider taking an advanced driver's course. Some car manufacturers also offer short courses if you buy a new car from them.



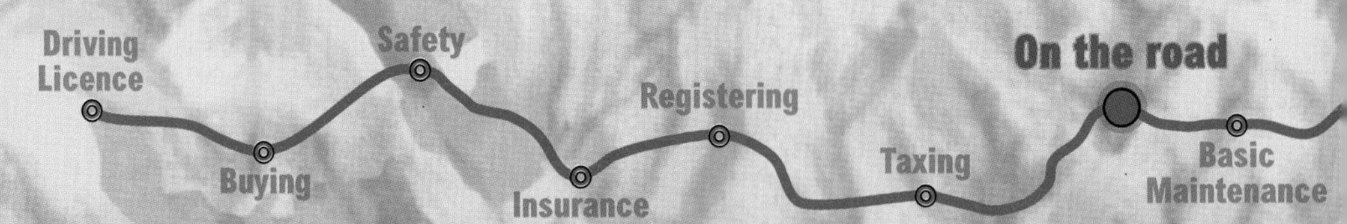

You should try to keep up to date with traffic regulations. Buy yourself a copy of *The Highway Code*. If it has been several years since you passed your test, yours could be out of date.

Highway Code

## Towing

towing

If you are considering towing a caravan or other trailer, think carefully about the choice of a suitable car. It is recommended that the weight of the trailer should not exceed 85 per cent of the unladen weight of the car, but check the driver's handbook – this should set out the maximum trailer weight specified for your vehicle. The car manufacturer will also specify the maximum downwards load (noseweight) which can be applied to the towing ball without overloading the rear axle. Noseweight can be checked with gauges available from accessory shops or by using bathroom scales and a suitable length of wood under the trailer coupling head.

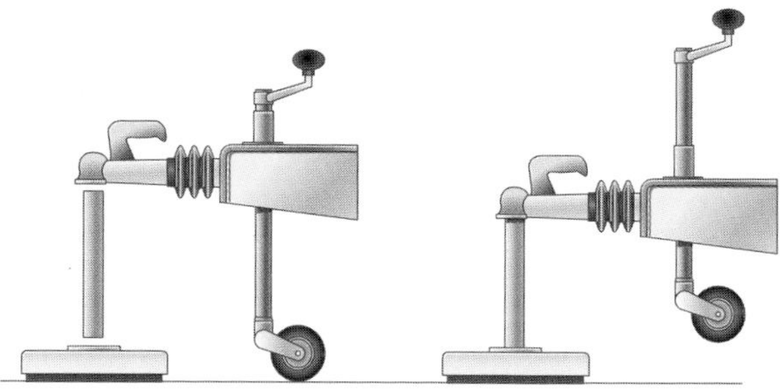

In addition to the main ball coupling, the car and trailer must also be connected either by a secondary coupling or breakaway cable, depending on the weight of the trailer and whether or not it is fitted with a braking system. In the case of most cars first registered after 1 August 1998, if a towbar is fitted at any time, the bar must be approved to European Community Directive 94/20/EC and will be 'e' marked.

## Passenger safety

the law

### Seat belts

Wearing a seat belt is the single most important action you can take to minimise your risk of death or injury in an accident. **Seat belts save lives.**

When you are in a car and you run into something, the car decelerates very quickly. Unless you are prevented from doing so by some form of restraint, such as a seat belt, you and the other people in the car, front and rear, keep on



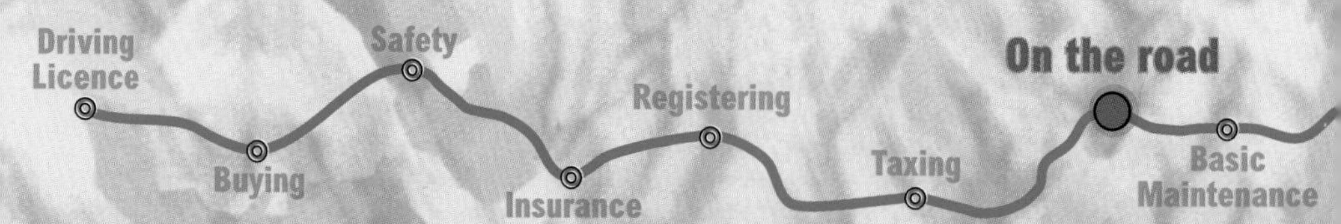

moving at roughly the speed the car was travelling before the impact.

In a crash at 30 mph, unless you wear a seat belt, you will hit whatever is in front of you with a force of between 30 and 60 times your own body weight. Such an impact is likely to result in death or serious injury.

Front seat occupants, if unrestrained, would smash their heads against the windscreen. Their bodies would plough into the steering wheel or dashboard and their legs could get crushed in the footwells. They could even be ejected from the car.

Unrestrained rear seat passengers would hurtle upwards and forwards and hit the back of the front seats and their occupants. They might clash heads with the front seat occupants or crush them, causing serious or fatal injuries to both themselves and the front seat occupants, even if the front seat occupants were wearing seat belts.

Seat belts and child restraints have been proved to reduce such injuries and to save lives, so use them.

When you are in a car that's been hit from behind it's a bit different. You and your car are suddenly forced to go forward at about the speed at which the car behind hits you. If your head is not supported it will be thrown backwards relative to your body. If there is a correctly adjusted head

restraint this does not happen. If there is no head restraint, or it is badly adjusted, very high forces are transmitted through your neck. It is these forces that cause what most people know as a whiplash injury.

No one would dream of going on a fairground ride without demanding proper safety harnesses. Yet the forces that make the fairground ride dangerous are much less than those acting on you in a crash.

| | Front seat (all vehicles) | Rear seat (cars and small minibuses*) | Whose responsibility |
|---|---|---|---|
| **Driver** | Must be worn if fitted | | Driver |
| **Child under 3 years old** | Appropriate child restraint must be worn | Appropriate child restraint must be worn if available | Driver |
| **Child aged 3 to 11 and under 1.5 metres (about 5 feet) in height** | Appropriate child restraint must be worn if available. If not, an adult seat belt must be worn | Appropriate child restraint must be worn if available. If not, an adult seat belt must be worn if available | Driver |
| **Child aged 12 or 13 or younger child 1.5 metres or more in height.** | Adult seat belt must be worn if available | Adult seat belt must be worn if available | Driver |
| **Passenger** over the age of 14 | Must be worn if available | Must be worn if available | Passenger |

* Minibuses with an unladen weight of 2540 kg or less.



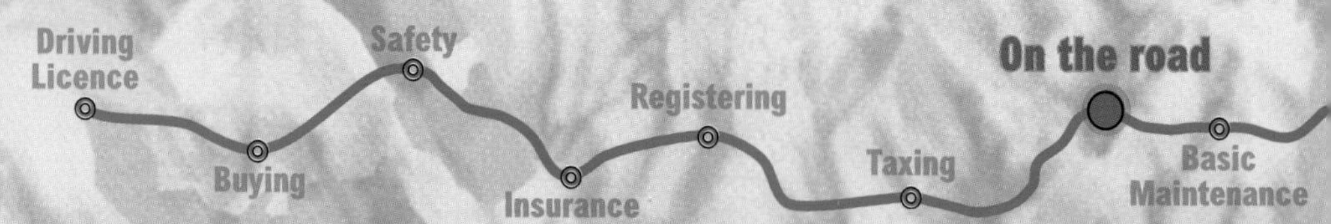

**Warning: never use a rear-facing child restraint in a seat which is protected by a front airbag.**

Modern cars will have three-point, lap and diagonal, seat belts on their front seats – these are designed to restrain both the upper and lower body.

Since April 1987, all new cars have had rear seat belts fitted as standard equipment. Some new cars will have lap and diagonal belts in all the rear seats. When considering rear seat belts, remember that lap belts are not as effective as lap-and-diagonal belts. However, they are still much safer than not wearing a belt at all.

Drivers or passengers with physical disabilities may need to use specially adapted belts known as 'disabled persons' belts'. Their design may differ from the standard lap or three-point seat belt and they are intended for use solely by disabled people.

## Wearing seat belts properly

proper use

When you put on a three-point belt, the lap portion should lie across your hips, not your stomach. The diagonal part should ideally be midway across your shoulder and should not touch your neck. Avoid using any clips or other 'comfort devices' to lock or reposition a seat belt as these may interfere with the operation of the belt. Lap belts should similarly lie across your hips, not across your stomach.

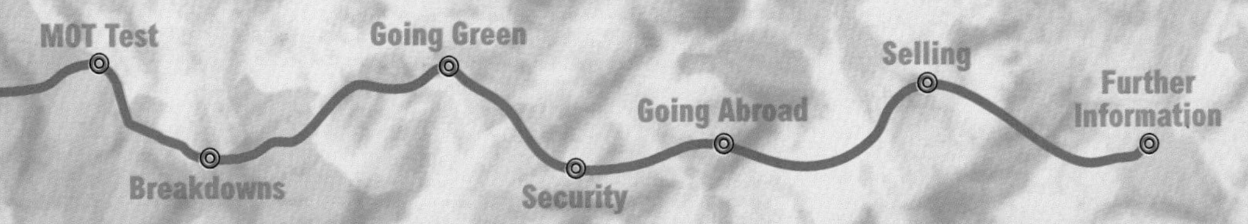

exemptions

It is important to minimise the amount of slack in the belt. In a severe crash, any slack can allow enough movement for you still to hit the steering wheel or dashboard. You could also slip out under the belt. Before you set off, whatever type of seat belt you are wearing, make sure that it has no slack.

airbags

## Airbags (for more information see chapter 3)

The speed and force of an inflating airbag may occasionally cause injuries, but these are generally minor compared with the injuries which might have occurred in a serious accident had an airbag not been present. However, serious or fatal injuries can be caused if an occupant is too close to an airbag when it inflates.

Drivers should always wear their seat belt, and sit as far back from the steering wheel as reasonably possible but make sure that proper control of the vehicle can still be maintained and all the instruments can be seen. Advice in the US and Canada is that the distance between the centre of the steering wheel and the breastbone should be at least 25 cm (10 inches). However, airbag systems differ from car to car so you should always check and follow the specific advice from the vehicle manufacturer.

Front seat passengers should also always wear their seat belt, sit well back and never put their feet on the dashboard or attach anything to the dashboard over or near the airbag.



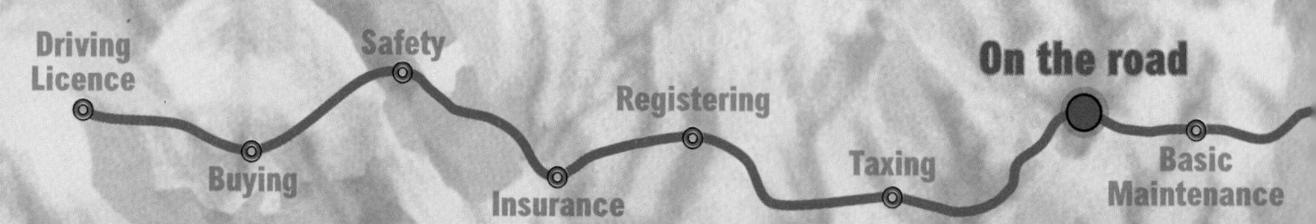

Where side airbags are fitted, always sit properly in the seat and do not lean close to or against the door. If the airbag is located in the seat, either don't fit seat covers at all or fit only specially designed covers recommended for the vehicle.

As explained previously, don't fit a rear-facing child seat in the passenger seat of a car which is protected by a front airbag.

Always follow the advice in the vehicle handbook, and if you have any doubts seek guidance from the vehicle manufacturer.

Airbags and their control systems don't need maintenance and should never be tampered with as they contain pressurised gas or an explosive – both of which have the potential to cause injury.

## Head restraints

Head restraints (commonly known as headrests) are provided for safety, not for comfort.

When you are in a car hit from behind your body is pushed forward. If your head is not supported it is thrown backwards relative to your body. This causes 'whiplash' injuries. Head restraints are designed to prevent this happening. Look for a car that has head restraints on all the seats, including those in the rear.

Whiplash injuries may not be life threatening, but can turn out to be very long term and painful. They are relatively easy to prevent, so it makes sense to choose a vehicle with good head restraints and to use them correctly.

For maximum protection the middle or rigid part of the head restraint should be at least as high as the eyes or the top of the ears and the head restraint should be as close to the back of the head as is comfortable. Many head restraints cannot be raised sufficiently high to offer good protection to the majority of occupants.

Head restraints essentially come in two types: adjustable and fixed:

- adjustable head restraints have to be adjusted manually for the individual occupant. Check the position of the head restraint every time you get in a car. Too often adjustable head restraints are left in their lowest position and don't give the desired protection.
- fixed head restraints are designed to give the right support for occupants of about average height, although taller occupants may find them too low.

The adjustable restraint shown opposite, on the left, would protect most people, even in the 'down' position. But the one on the right, if in the lowest position, would protect only the shortest people. Therefore the best choice would be a good adjustable (left) or fixed head restraint (centre) which extends sufficiently high.

## Child restraints



Children still die or are seriously injured in car accidents because they are not properly restrained. Don't think you can simply hold onto your child in an accident – you can't. The forces involved are just too great. You can best protect your children by putting them in a purpose made child restraint which is appropriate for their weight, size and age. Sitting them on ordinary household cushions or folded blankets so that they can use an adult seat belt will not give the same level of protection. Make sure children are properly restrained every time they travel in a car.

### Choosing child restraints

Child restraints are available in a wide variety of types – baby seats, child seats, booster seats and booster cushions – and they must carry the United Nations 'E' mark, the European 'e' mark or BS 'Kitemark'.



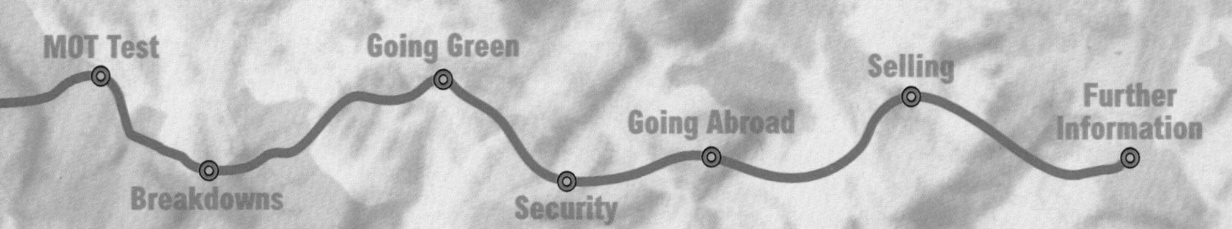

The appropriate restraint depends on the weight, size and age of your child. Below is a table giving the approximate ages and weights of children for which the different types of child restraint are appropriate. However, you should always refer to the packaging and manufacturers instructions for information about the suitability of a particular restraint for your child.

| Child restraint type | Weight range | Age range (approx) |
|---|---|---|
| Baby seat | Up to 10 kg * (22 lb) | Birth to 9 months |
| Child seat | 9 kg to 18 kg (20-40 lb) | 6 months to 4years |
| Booster seat | 9 kg to 25 kg (20-55 lb) | 6 months to 6 years |
| Booster cushion | 15 kg to 36 kg (33-80 lb) | 4 years to 11 years |

•*Some baby seats may be suitable for children up to 13kg (15 months approx).*

Child restraints are generally secured by the adult belt fitted in the car. Before buying a child restraint you should try it in your car to make sure it can be fitted properly. A properly installed restraint should be firm, with no excessive forward or sideways movement. The buckle of the adult seat belt



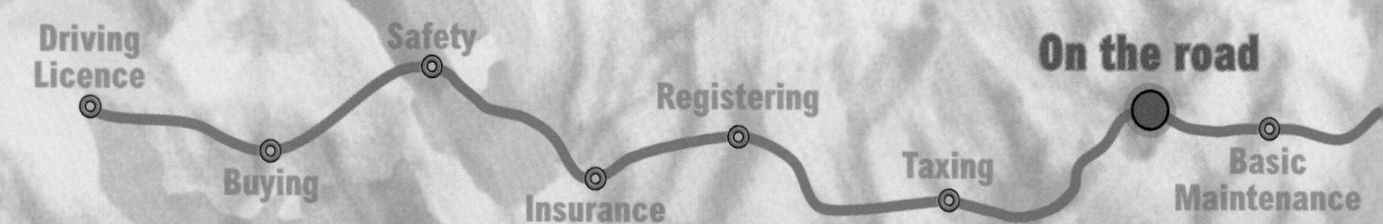

should not rest on the frame, as it may break in an accident. If you are in any doubt try an alternative design of restraint, or see whether the manufacturer is able to recommend a special fitting kit.

Make sure you understand how to fit the restraint properly and always follow the manufacturer's instructions. Allow time to fit child restraints each time you use the car – several minutes if necessary. Keep the instructions somewhere safe for future reference.

Also make sure that you know how to adjust the harness properly – you should not be able to fit more than two fingers under the harness your child is wearing.

Beware of old or second-hand baby and child restraints as they may be damaged, worn out or have parts missing and may not have the correct fitting instructions. They may also not meet the latest safety standards.

Although child restraints can be used in the front or rear of a car, on balance children will be safer in the rear – the safest place being in the centre of the rear seat as long as a suitable adult seat belt is available to secure the restraint.

Never put your child in the luggage space of hatchbacks or estate cars unless the vehicle is equipped with a restraint specifically designed for that purpose.

## Baby seats

For a very young child this is the safest type of restraint available. Baby seats are rear-facing so that the baby's weak neck can be safely supported.

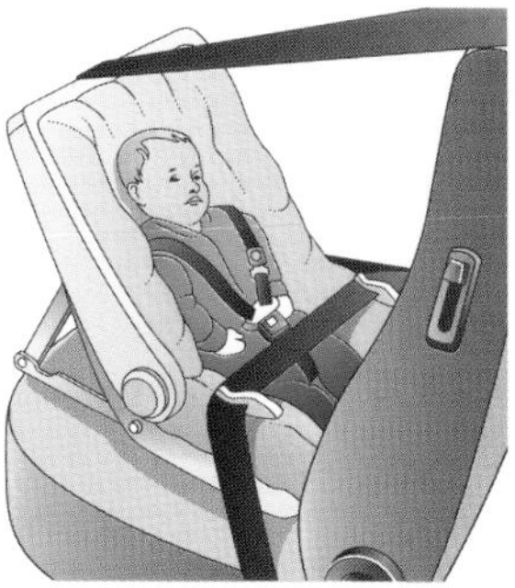

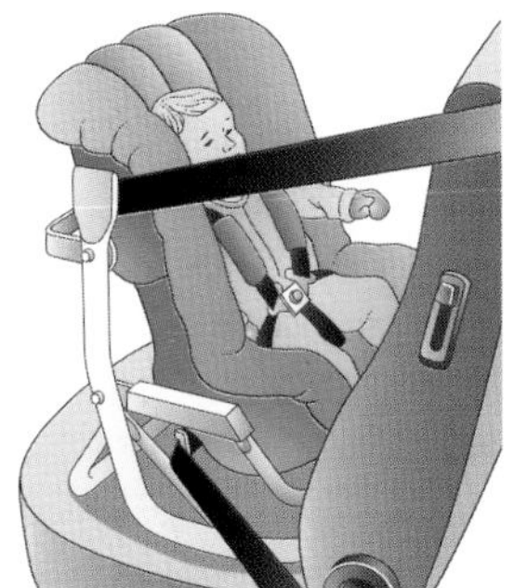

They can be fitted in the car using the adult lap-and-diagonal seat belt. If the baby seat is convenient to use and to carry you are more likely to use it on every journey.

Never use a rear-facing child restraint in a seat which is protected by a front airbag. This is because the seat is positioned so close to the dashboard that the expanding airbag is likely to cause serious or fatal injury.

Some baby seats can be converted into forward-facing child seats and used until your child is about four years old. You should not put a child into a forward-facing child seat until they are at least nine months old and can sit up unaided for a prolonged period.



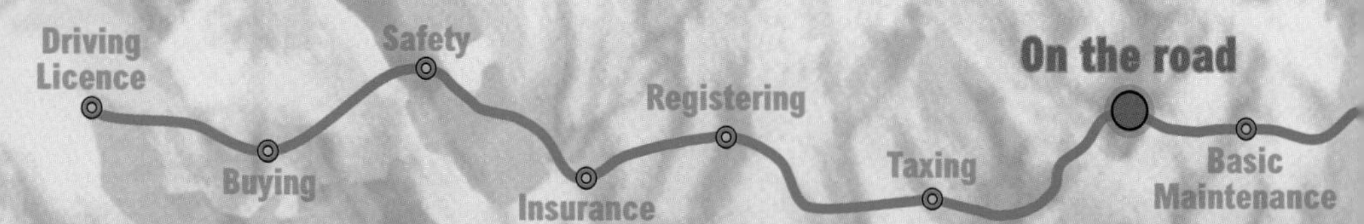

## Child seats

Child seats are in the form of a separately framed seat. The child seat is secured in the vehicle by an adult seat belt or by its own special retention straps. The child is then restrained in the seat by the seat's integral harness. The framed child seat has the advantage of having a harness specifically designed for a child in that age group.

A child seat harness should include a crotch strap which will prevent the child from sliding out feet first under the belt during an accident.

## Booster seats

A booster seat raises and positions a child so that an adult seat belt can be used effectively. It incorporates guides which the seat belt should pass through, ensuring that the adult seat belt is correctly positioned. Both the booster seat and the child are restrained by the adult seat belt.

Booster seats are generally easy to install correctly, as long as a lap-and-diagonal seat belt is available. They should not be used when only a lap belt is fitted, unless they are specifically designed to do so.

### Booster cushions

These are intended for children who are too large for a child seat. They are designed to raise the child so that an adult seat belt can be used safely. A booster cushion should be used until the child is tall enough to wear an adult seat belt in the correct way.

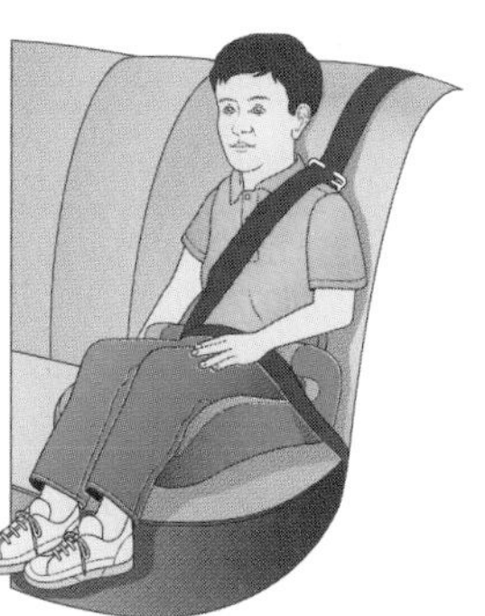

A booster cushion with a guide strap to improve the position of the shoulder belt is best.



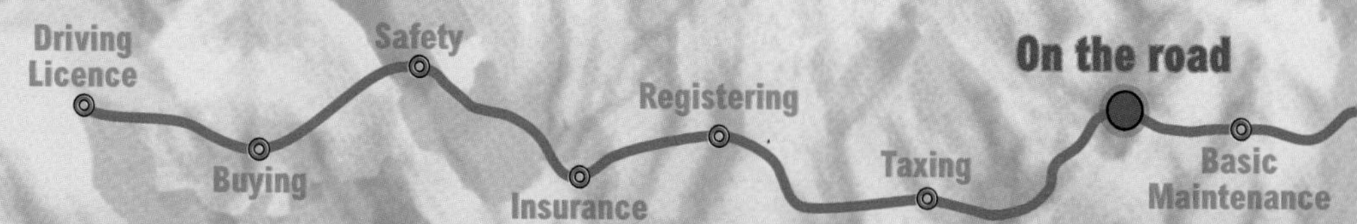

### Carrycots

Carrycots with restraint straps are not designed to withstand the considerable forces generated in an accident. A baby seat is safer and more convenient than a carrycot, although doctors may occasionally advise the use of carrycots, e.g. for premature babies. The best advice is that carrycots should be used only if the alternative is for your child to travel without any type of restraint at all.

## Carrying loads

In the same way that rear seat passengers should wear seat belts partly to protect the people in front you should always try to strap loads down to prevent them hurtling forward in a frontal accident. In a crash at only 30 mph, any unrestrained load will hit whatever is in front of it with a force of between 30 and 60 times its normal weight. The folding rear seats in hatchbacks and estates, especially split seats, are rarely strong enough to hold back heavy loads in a severe frontal accident. Saloons with non-folding seats are more likely to prevent this dangerous shifting of heavy loads.

The 'parcel shelf' should be kept clear because, in an accident, items on it, such as packages, umbrellas or even dogs (and it has happened!) can cause serious injuries.



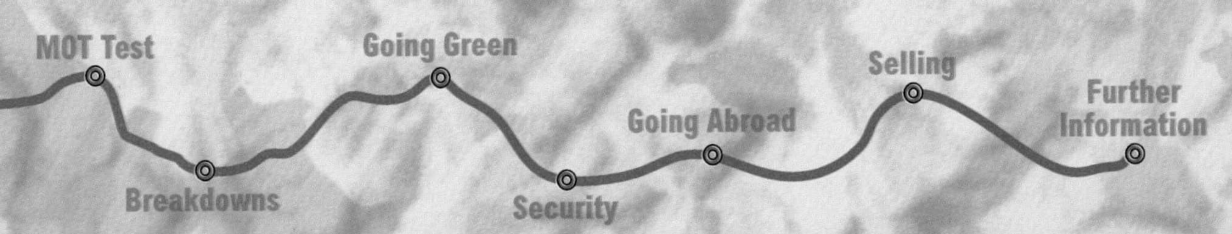

People who wish to transport objects of over around 25 kg (55 lbs), such as a sack of potatoes, should look for cars fitted with tie-down eyes, small loops attached to the floor or side panels, although only a few manufacturers fit them. Tie-down eyes are particularly useful to people who use a car for business purposes to carry heavy merchandise or equipment.

If tie-downs are not available, it is recommended that you fasten the rear seat belts, even if there are no occupants in the seat. This will help to hold the seat back in place and to restrain the load.

Some safety-conscious manufacturers are now fitting stronger folding backrests for the rear seats. These not only restrain the load but also provide an upper anchorage for a three-point seat belt for the centre rear seat.



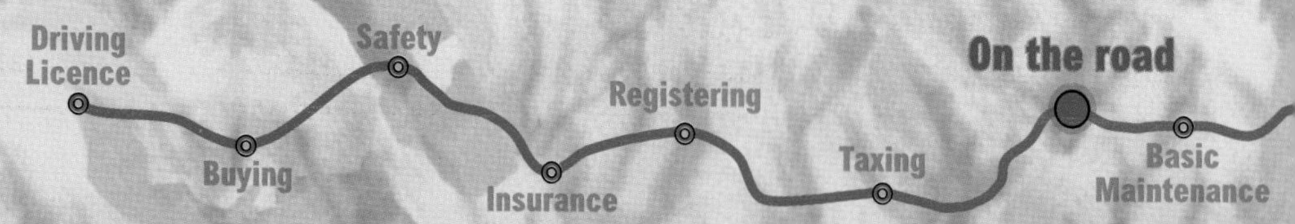

## Lights

All vehicles must be fitted with position lamps (sidelights), dipped beam and main beam headlamps and direction indicators showing to the front. The colour of these lamps, when lit, should be white, except the direction indicators which must be amber. No lamp on the front of a vehicle should ever show a red light to the front.

Vehicles must also be fitted with reflectors, position lamps, brake lights, fog lamps and direction indicators showing to the rear. The colour of these must be red, except the direction indicators which must be amber.

Position lights must be used between sunset and sunrise.

Dipped-beam headlamps must be used:

- from half an hour after sunset to half an hour before sunrise except on a well lit road with a 30 mph speed limit; and
- in seriously reduced visibility.

Front fog lamps can be used only in seriously reduced visibility.

### Dazzle

Highway Code

Be considerate of other road users and remember that even though you cannot see your lights they may be causing



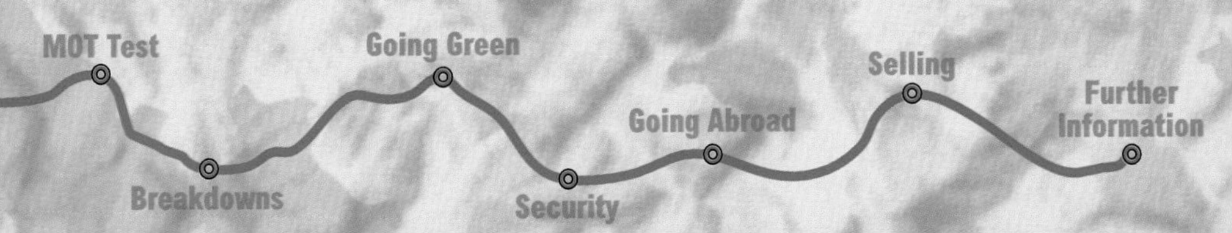

dazzle to other road users. Do not use your lights unnecessarily.

When your vehicle is loaded, or towing a heavy trailer, the headlamps usually require adjusting; on some cars this can be done from the driver's seat. Badly adjusted headlamps either dazzle other road users or give you a limited view of the road ahead. If in doubt, ask your garage to reset your headlamps.

Apply the handbrake when you are stationary for any period of time in a traffic queue so that the stop lamp does not stay on.



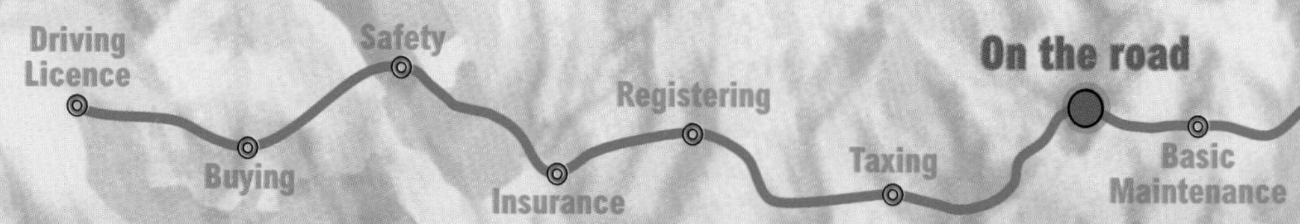

## Fog lamps and driving lamps

For information on fog lamps, see chapter 8 under "lights'.

Driving lamps should only be used when there are no other road users in front of your vehicle. Remember, it can be just as dazzling to have bright lights shining in your mirrors as it is to have them coming towards you. See chapter 8 under "lights' for more information.

## Hazard warning lamps

These must only be used when your vehicle is either stationary and causing an obstruction, or on a motorway or unrestricted dual carriageway to warn of an obstruction ahead. Their use does not entitle you to stop in places where restrictions are in force, e.g. on double yellow lines.

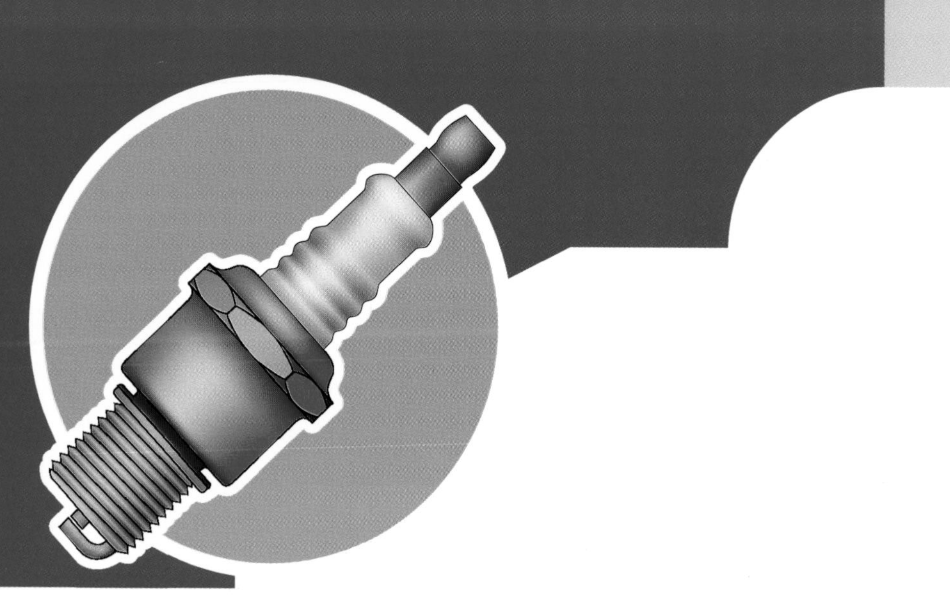

chapter eight

# basic maintenance

looking after your car
engine
steering
suspension
brakes
tyres
battery
lights
things to remember

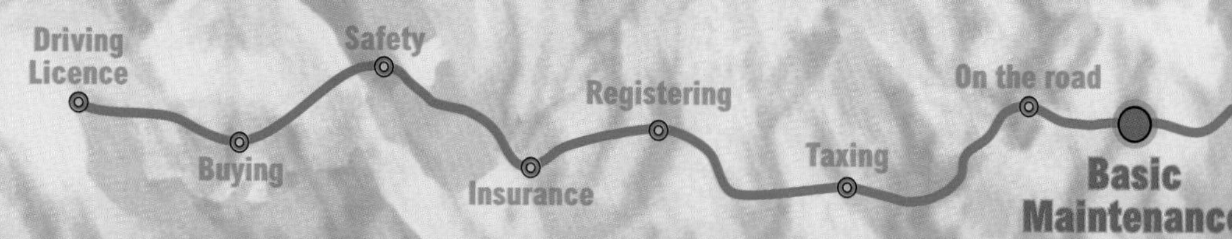

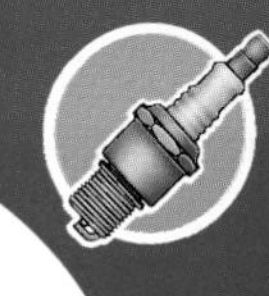

## Looking after your car

garage service advice

Routine checks of the oil, fuel, water, tyres and tyre pressures, particularly before a long journey, can help save trouble and expense and prolong the life of your car. You'll find that regular service checks on brakes and engine by a qualified mechanic can also save time and money.

Neglecting the maintenance of vital controls, such as brakes and steering, is dangerous.

Oil is necessary to lubricate your engine. You need to keep the oil at the level recommended by the vehicle manufacturer. Check regularly and top up the oil when necessary, especially before a long journey.

Your car is your responsibility and you should ensure it is always properly maintained in a roadworthy condition. Don't wait for your annual MOT or a breakdown to repair it.

## Engine

### How to check the oil level

Ensure the vehicle is on a level area, not on a slope, and has been stationary for a while. Look for the dipstick on the engine block of your vehicle.



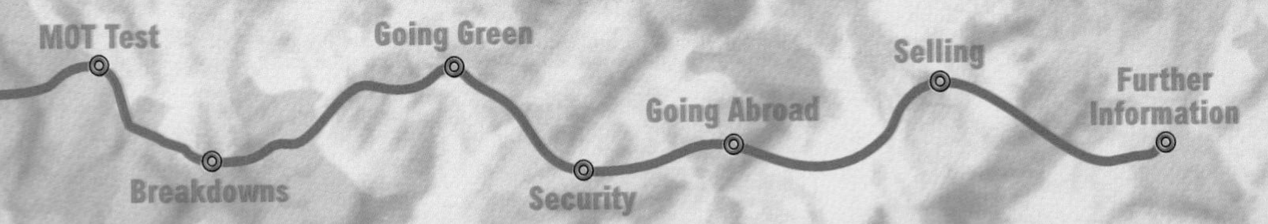

The dipstick will tell you the amount of oil in the engine. See the vehicle handbook.

You should check the oil while the engine is cold for a more accurate result. You'll need a clean, dry cloth to wipe the dipstick.

Take particular care if your vehicle is fitted with automatic transmission. There may be an additional dipstick for transmission oil level checks. Consult the vehicle handbook.

oil care code

## Oil changes

Observe manufacturer's recommendations. If a large number of short journeys are involved, change the oil at more frequent intervals, especially in dusty conditions. Remember to have the oil filter changed at the same time.

**Warning:** oil is toxic and can cause skin problems. Wash oil off your hands immediately. Use protective gloves or barrier cream and always wash your hands immediately. Keep containers storing oil out of reach of children.



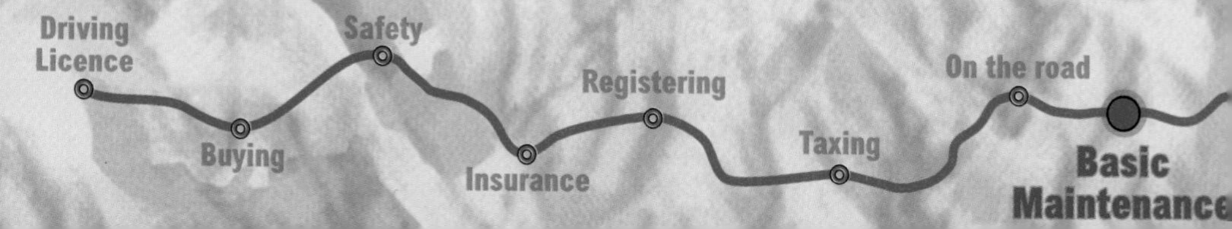

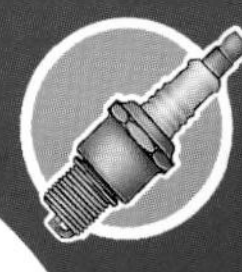

The amount of oil an engine will use depends on

- the type of engine
- the amount of wear
- how you drive.

Don't

- run the engine when the oil level is below the minimum mark
- add so much oil that the level rises above the maximum mark. You'll create excess pressure that could damage the engine seals and gaskets, and cause oil leaks. Moving internal parts can hit the oil surface in an overfull engine and may do serious damage.

## Warning light

If the oil pressure warning light on your instrument panel comes on when you're driving, this indicates a pressure failure. Stop as soon as you can and check the oil level.

## Lubricating oils – engine

The oil in your engine has to perform several tasks at high pressures and temperatures up to 300°C. It helps to

- resist wear on the moving surfaces
- combat the corrosive acids formed as the hydrocarbons in the fuels are burnt in the engine
- keep the engine cool.



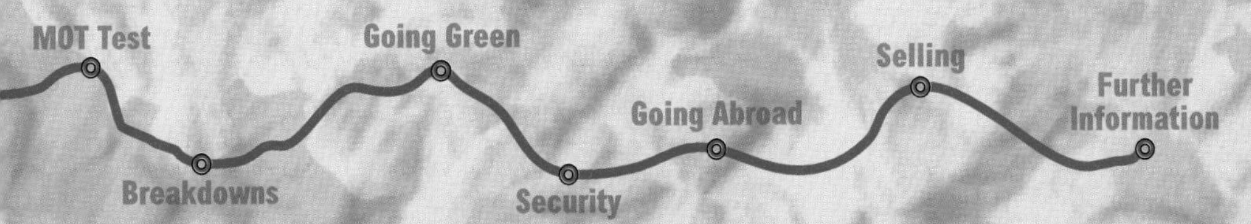

It also has to withstand gradual contamination from both fuel and dirt.

Make sure you always use the lubricants recommended in the handbook.

## Lubricating oils – gearbox

Most vehicles have a separate lubricating oil supply for the gearbox. This oil is especially formulated for use in the gearbox and you should always follow the instructions in the vehicle handbook.

It's not necessary to drain the gearbox in most cases, but the level should be checked at service intervals.

## Lubricating oils – final drive/rear axle

Front-wheel drive vehicles may not have a separate supply for the final drive and gearbox, but most have a common filler/level plug, and the specified gear oil should be used to top up. With rear-wheel drive vehicles, there's a filler/level hole at the rear of the differential (on the rear axle) which can be more easily reached when the vehicle is raised, but remember to keep the vehicle level. It's important that the correct hypoid-type EP (Extreme Pressure) oil specified in the vehicle handbook is used. You may have to squeeze the top-up oil in via a plastic bottle and tube.



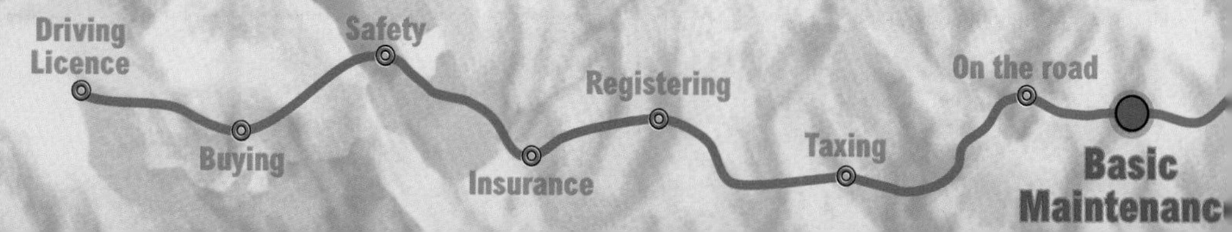

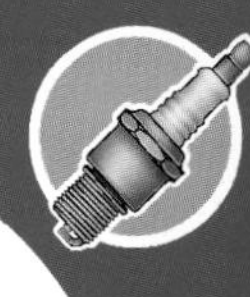

## Coolant

Vehicles today use a mixture of water and anti-freeze to make up the coolant as this helps to keep most engines comparatively cool, and is kept in the radiator all the year round.

The anti-freeze contains a corrosion inhibitor which reduces rust oxidation in alloy engines and it prolongs the life of the system. In cold weather, maintain the recommended strength of anti-freeze. Have it checked annually.

You should frequently check the coolant level, particularly before a long trip, topping up with coolant as necessary. The need to top up often might indicate a leak or other fault in the cooling system. Have it checked by your garage/dealer.

It's a good idea always to carry a supply of coolant with you. Look for the high/low level markings on the header tank where one is fitted.

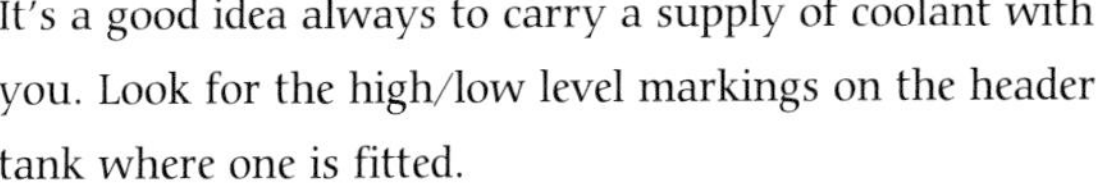

**Warning:**

- never remove a radiator cap when the engine is hot
- never add cold water to an overheated engine. Let it cool for a while first
- don't overfill the system as the excess will blow as soon as it warms up.

### Air filter

Replace the air filter at the intervals recommended by the manufacturer, or sooner if the vehicle is used in exceptionally dusty conditions.

### Overhead camshaft engines

On this design of engine it is vital to replace the camshaft drive belt at the recommended intervals. Serious damage can be caused to the engine if the belt breaks.

## Steering

Excessive movement or play in the steering wheel may indicate wear in the steering mechanism. If you feel or hear any knocking or rattling noises from the steering or suspension you should seek qualified advice without delay.

### Power-assisted steering (PAS) pump reservoir

Check the level of fluid regularly when the engine is switched off. The level should be between the 'min' and 'max' marks.

Never run the engine without oil in the pump reservoir. You could severely damage the pump or cause it to seize up completely.



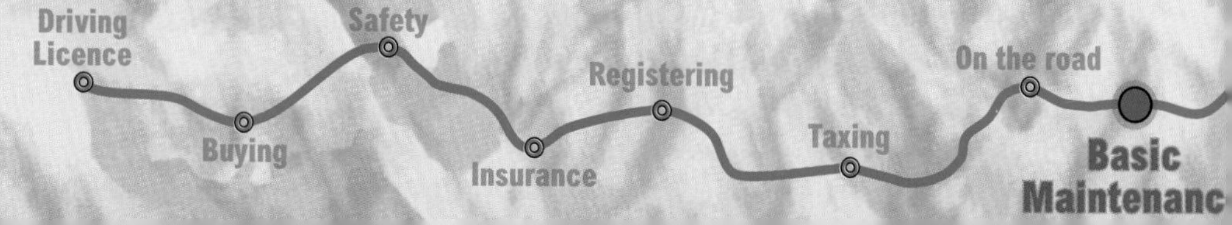

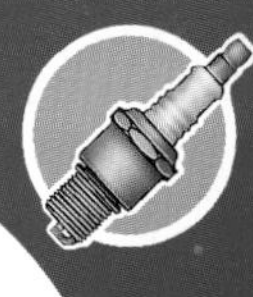

## Suspension

Check the condition of shock absorbers by examining them for signs of fluid leaks and by bouncing the vehicle. The test is to bounce each corner of the vehicle and it should not continue to bounce unduly when released. If in doubt, seek qualified assistance.

Remember, worn shock absorbers make a vehicle difficult to control and can increase your stopping distance.

## Brakes

Brakes are one of the most important elements in driving safety.

### Footbrake

Note any variations in braking efficiency. If the brakes feel spongy or slack, get them checked by a qualified mechanic. They are too important to be ignored.

### Testing your brakes

Test the brakes every day as you set out. Choose a safe spot on the road.

If you hear any strange noises, or if the vehicle pulls to one side, consult your garage immediately.

Check the brake fluid level regularly but don't overfill. Look out for the high/low markings on the reservoir.

Make sure the brake fluid reservoir is kept topped up. Consult the handbook.

### Handbrake

Adjust the handbrake setting if

- the amount of travel is above the limit specified in the handbook
- the vehicle can roll on a gradient when the handbrake is fully set.

### Regular servicing

Regular servicing will help to make sure your brakes are safe. Follow the manufacturer's recommendation on service intervals.

Unless you're an enthusiastic and skilled amateur mechanic, leave brake checking, adjustment and replacement of pads and shoes to your garage.

If you're in any doubt about your vehicle's ability to brake safely, don't use it. Have it checked immediately.

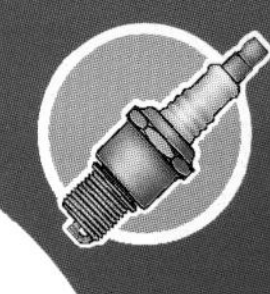

Most vehicles are equipped with a warning signal to indicate certain faults within the braking system. If the red warning signal shows, consult your vehicle handbook or obtain guidance from a competent mechanic. Driving the vehicle with a brake defect could be dangerous and may constitute an offence.

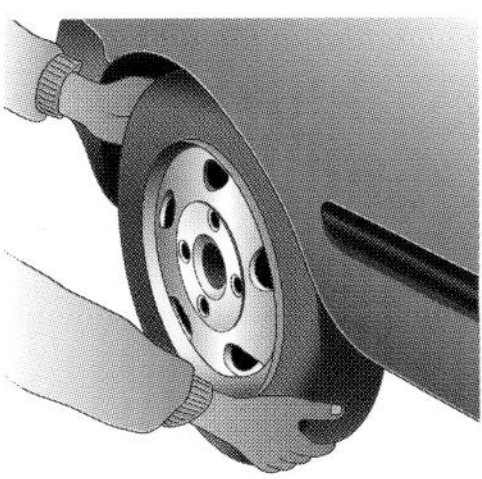

### Anti-lock braking systems (ABS)

If your vehicle has anti-lock brakes, there will also be a warning light for that system. The ABS goes through a self check when the ignition is switched on. If the light comes on at any other time it indicates a fault. Have the system checked immediately. Consult your vehicle handbook or your garage **before** driving the vehicle. Only if it's safe, drive carefully to the nearest garage.

## Tyres



Your tyres are your only contact with the road. The area of contact is as small as the sole of a shoe for each tyre. Tyres



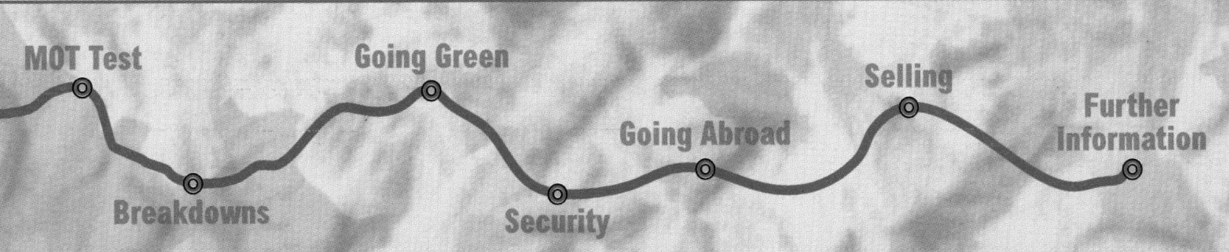

won't grip properly and safely unless they're in good condition and correctly inflated. They can easily become damaged. Make sure you check wear and tear and replace them when necessary.

The penalties for using faulty tyres or tyres worn beyond the minimum legal tread depth are very severe. They may include a fixed fine up to £2500, discretionary disqualification and driving licence endorsement, for every faulty tyre.

When you check the condition of your tyres:

- check that the walls of the tyres are free from cuts and bulges. Don't forget the inner walls (i.e., those facing each other under the car)
- check that all your tyres have a good depth of tread right across and all around them. The legal requirement for cars, vans and trailers/caravans is not less than 1.6 mm tread depth across the central three-quarters of the breadth of the tyre and around the entire outer circumference
- have the wheel alignment and wheel balance, suspension and braking system checked. If there's a fault, get it put right as soon as you can, otherwise the wear on the tyres will be excessive or uneven
- if you see that some parts of the tread are wearing before others it could indicate a tyre, brake, steering or suspension fault.

Don't let grease and oil stay on your tyres. Remove anything (stones, glass, etc.) caught in the treads. These can work their way in and cause damage.

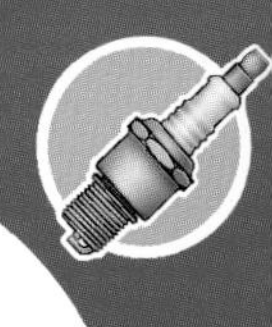



## Tyre pressures

You can't guess pressures just by looking at a tyre, except when it's obviously flat. Check your tyres regularly – at least once a week. Use a reliable gauge and follow the manufacturer's guide for the correct tyre pressure.

Check your tyres and adjust the pressure when they're cold. Don't forget the spare tyre. Remember to refit the valve caps.

The vehicle handbook will also tell you if you need different pressures for different conditions. Generally, the pressure should be higher for a heavily loaded vehicle or if you're intending to drive at high speed for a long distance, e.g. on motorway journeys.

Remember, it is so dangerous that it's an offence to use a car with a tyre not properly inflated.

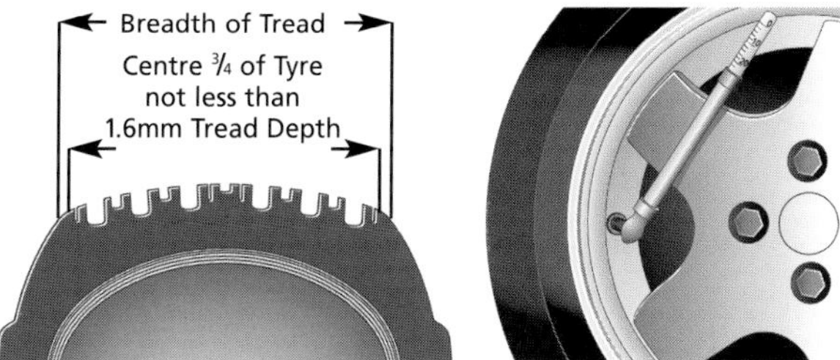


## Replacing tyres

You'll need to distinguish between the two main types of tyre in general use: cross-ply and radial-ply. In cross-ply



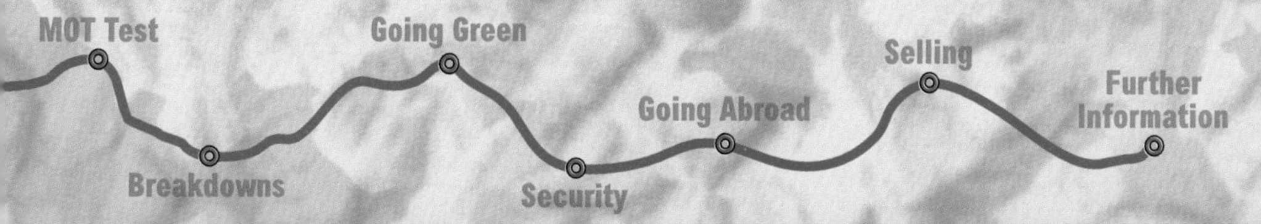

tyres the cords making up the structure of the tyre run diagonally across it, with alternate layers at opposite angles, forming a trellis structure. In radial-ply tyres the cords run at right angles across the tyre, resulting in thinner and more flexible walls. The tread of a radial-ply tyre gives extra grip in the wet because of the way it's structured. Most modern cars are fitted with radial-ply tyres.

The type of tyre is indicated on the sidewall markings. In the case of radial-ply tyres the letter 'R' is part of the tyre size marking as in the example below and, in addition, the word 'radial' may be shown on the sidewall.

Example: 175/65 R14 82T

Cross-ply tyres normally do not have any identification marking but some examples may have the letter 'D' in place of 'R'.

### Mixing tyres

It's an offence to put radial-ply tyres at the front with cross-ply at the rear. There are no exceptions to this rule. It applies whether the vehicle has front or rear-wheel drive. It's also an offence to mix cross- and radial-ply tyres on the same axle.

Mixing radial and cross-ply tyres makes rotating tyres, where it's recommended for your vehicle, difficult if not

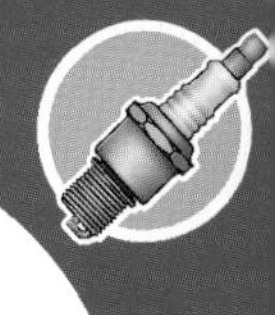

impossible. If you want to change the type, change all the tyres, including the spare. Keep to the same type all round: all cross-ply or all radial. If you can't avoid mixing types, then make sure the radial-ply tyres go on the back. The car will handle differently from the way it would with the same type of tyres all round.

Get the advice of a tyre expert if you're changing type. Good garages and specialist tyre services know the regulations; ask them.

safe disposal

## Tubeless tyres

When you're replacing a tubeless tyre, fit a new valve to the wheel.

tyres

Punctures should be properly repaired to restore the air retention properties of the tyre, for example in accordance with British Standard BS AU 159. A tube should not be fitted to a tubeless tyre to cure a puncture and is not recommended for use in a tyre having a profile, or aspect ratio, less than '70'.

You should run in new tyres at reasonable speeds for the first 100 miles (160 kilometres) because they don't grip the road surface quite so well when they are new and shiny.



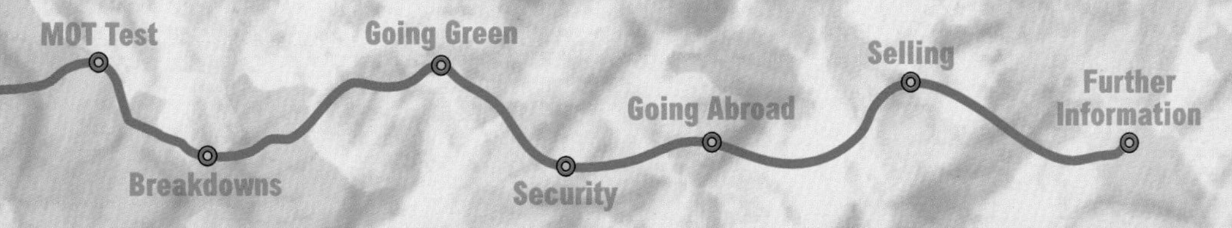

**To save wear and tear on tyres:**

- maintain correct, recommended, pressures
- avoid driving over potholes and broken road surfaces. If you can't avoid them, slow down
- don't drive over kerbs or scrape the wheels along them when manoeuvring. You'll damage the wall of the tyre and this could cause a blow-out later
- hitting the kerb can also affect the tracking of the front wheels. If there are any signs of uneven front tyre wear, have the steering checked
- think and plan ahead. Avoid high speeds, fast cornering and heavy braking, all of which increase tyre wear.

## Battery

Some modern batteries are maintenance-free and sealed for life. The terminals should be secure, clean and greased.

When the battery is fitted with a filler cap or caps, check the level of the fluid. The plates in each cell should be covered. Top up with distilled water if necessary, but avoid overfilling.

## Lights

Check the operation of the front and rear lights, brake lights and indicators, including hazard lights, each time you use



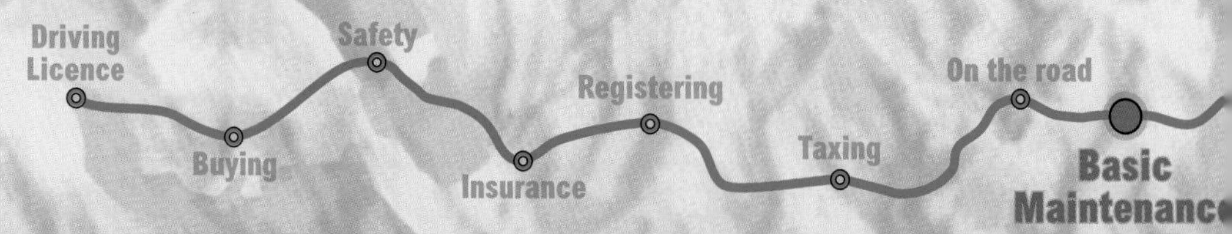

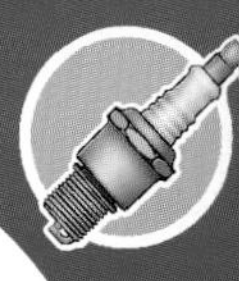

the vehicle. All lights must be clean, in good working order, and show a steady light. Direction indicators must flash between one and two times per second.

Make use of reflections in windows and garage doors, or ask someone to help you.

It's a good idea to carry a selection of spare bulbs. See your vehicle's owner's handbook for the bulb replacement procedure. If a headlamp bulb is replaced, the alignment can be affected and should be checked.

Headlights must be properly adjusted to

- avoid dazzling other road users
- enable the driver to see the road ahead adequately.

Check that the tell-tale lights indicating that a lamp has been switched on are working.



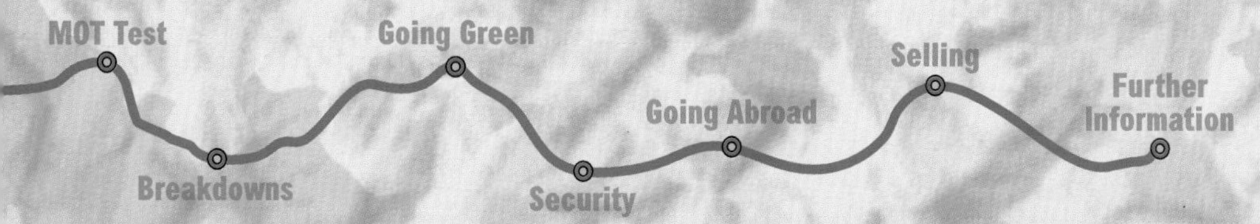

## Fog lamps and driving lamps

(see also chapter 7, 'lights')

Front fog lamps or driving lamps do not have to be fitted, but they may provide some benefits in certain circumstances.

Do not switch on front or rear fog lamps just because it's dark or raining. It is illegal to use them unless visibility is seriously reduced – generally less than 100 m (110 yds). Remember to switch them off at all other times because they don't make you more visible, all they do is dazzle other road users, and because of that can actually cause an accident. Make sure that you are able to switch them off easily when not needed.

Rear fog lamps must have a light on the dashboard to indicate when they are switched on. Check that it is located where you can see it. It is also a good idea to have one fitted to the front fog lamps, so that you do not leave them on by mistake.

Similarly, it is an offence to use driving lamps when they are likely to cause dazzle or discomfort to other road users. Driving lamps must be wired into the main beam headlamp circuit so that they can only be operated at the same time as the main beam headlamps.

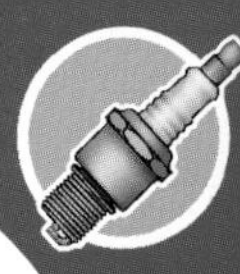

### Brake lights

Research has shown that separate (as opposed to combined) brake lights and rear position lamps – as on some current models – can help following drivers respond more quickly to brake signals. There are similar advantages in having a third brake light located away from the other rear lights, usually mounted centrally and fairly high up.

### Indicators

- must be clearly visible and in good working order
- must flash between one and two times per second.

## Things to remember

### Windscreen washers and wipers

Check the windscreen washer mechanism and the washer reservoirs. Make sure there's enough liquid. The washer can be very important in wet, muddy conditions. In winter add specially formulated screenwash to prevent the water freezing. If you carry a supply of water, you can use a sponge to wash away any heavy dirt wherever you happen to be. Check the wipers and replace worn or damaged blades.



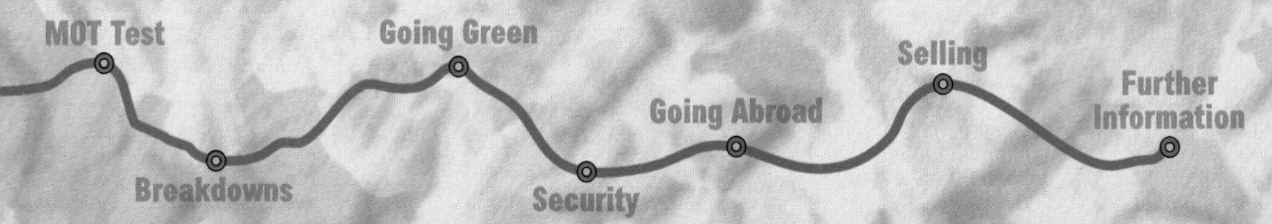

If your vehicle is fitted with headlight washers, the same attention should be paid to these.

## Horn

Check the horn is working properly and sounding clearly. Take care not to alarm or annoy others when doing so.

## Basic fault finding

For detailed advice, consult either the vehicle handbook, a workshop maintenance manual or a qualified mechanic.

If you have any doubts about the roadworthiness of the vehicle, obtain specialised assistance without delay. Don't ignore the warning signs.

Some minor faults can be easily identified and corrected comparatively simply, but with the more complex engine management and electronic systems in modern motor vehicles, anything beyond a simple repair is better left to qualified mechanics, especially when the vehicle's warranty might be affected.

TRL reports

The Transport Research Laboratory (TRL) periodically issues reports concerning transport. Check out the website.



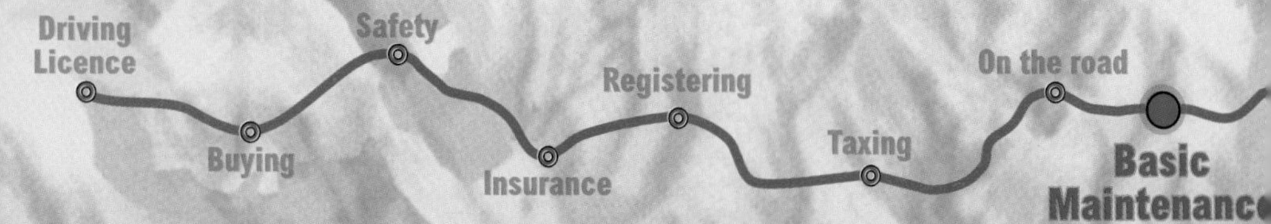

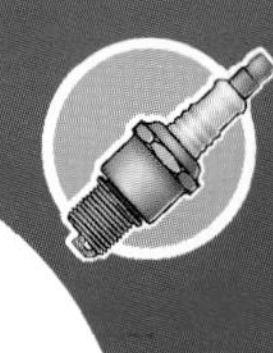

## The environment

waste management

Badly maintained cars use more fuel and emit more exhaust fumes. Your car should be regularly tuned and maintained, especially if it is an older model. If you are going to maintain your vehicle yourself you should not dispose of any dirty oil down the drain. This will pollute the water system. Take it to a service station or local authority site for recycling.

Do not pour anti-freeze into the water system – it is poisonous to fish, wildlife and people.

Dispose of old batteries, oil and used tyres at a local authority site.



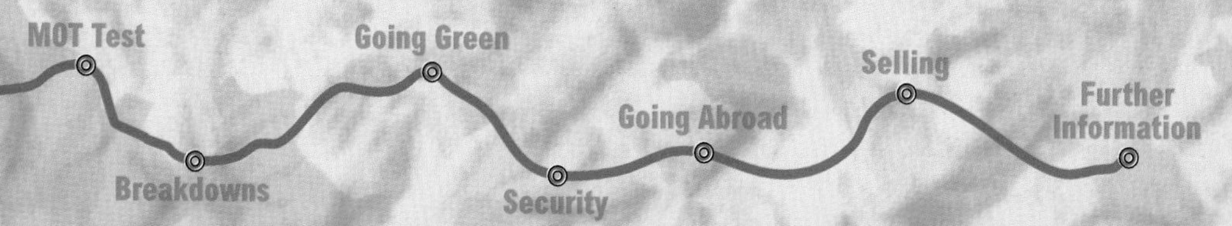

chapter nine

# the mot test

statutory requirements

what the test includes

if your car fails

frequently asked questions

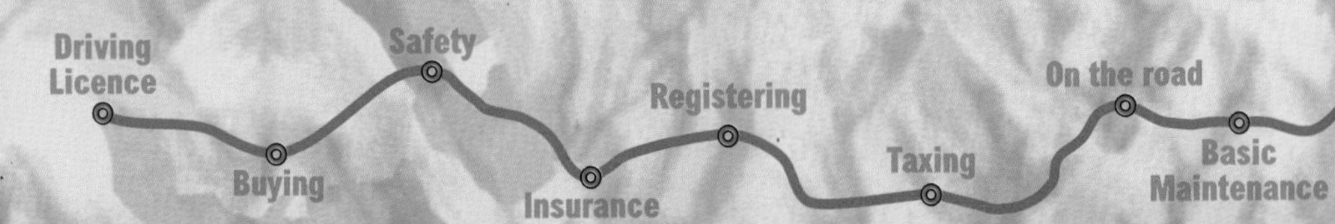

## Statutory requirements

If your car is three years or older it must have a current MOT certificate. You will not to be able to renew your Vehicle Excise Licence (tax disc) without it.

The purpose of the MOT test is to ensure that your vehicle meets key roadworthiness and environmental standards. It does not however, replace regular servicing.

The test must be carried out every year by a vehicle testing station appointed by the Vehicle Inspectorate (VI), an Executive Agency of the Department of Environment, Transport and the Regions.

### Testing time

computerisation

You can have your vehicle tested as much as one month before the current certificate runs out. The expiry date of the new certificate will be one year after the expiry date of the old one.

Please note that the following types of vehicle must be tested one year after registration and annually thereafter:

- lorries over 3,500 kg design gross weight
- buses with more than eight passenger seats
- ambulances
- taxis

Note that all these are tested under the MOT scheme.



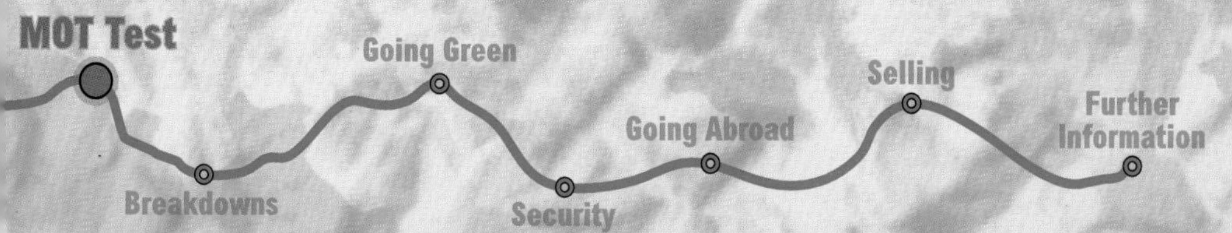

## What the test includes

The MOT tester will include a check on the

- seats: these should be secure and not liable to move through sudden braking
- lights: condition and operation: that they are secure and show the correct colour. Headlamps will also be checked to see if the aim is correct
- suspension: no components should be broken or bent, road springs are checked for condition
- steering: wheel is securely attached to the steering shaft
- brakes: condition, operation and performance (efficiency test). Note that the wheels are not removed
- tyres and wheels: condition, security, tyres size/type and tread depth
- seat belts: correct type, condition and operation
- registration plates: condition, security, digits correctly formed and spaced
- fuel system: no leaks, cap fastens securely and seals correctly
- doors: that all latch securely, that front doors open from inside and out; rear doors may need to open for the test to be carried out
- mirrors: present, good condition, secure, with good adjustment
- vehicle structure: free from excessive damage or corrosion in specified areas, no sharp edges
- exhaust system: secure, complete, without serious leaks and silences effectively
- exhaust emissions: vehicle meets the requirements for exhaust gas emissions. There are prescribed emission limits for petrol-engined vehicles registered from1 August 1975 and the MOT test will check that these limits are not exceeded

- horn: correct operation and the right type
- wipers/washer: operates to give the driver a clear view ahead
- Vehicle Identification Number (VIN): not more than one different VIN is present and legible on or after 1 August 1980
- windscreen: condition, driver's view of the road.

## If your car fails

If your vehicle fails and you want to continue to use it, you must make arrangements to have the necessary repairs carried out without delay. The vehicle must pass an MOT test before it's used on the road except when

- driving it away from the testing station after failing the test
- driving to have the repairs carried out where previous arrangements have been made
- driving to an MOT test appointment booked in advance.

Even in these circumstances you can still be prosecuted if your car is not roadworthy under the various regulations governing its construction and use. In addition, check that your insurance cover remains valid.

The test relates only to the condition of the testable items at the time of the test. It should not be regarded as evidence of the condition of the items tested at any other time nor should it be taken as evidence of the general mechanical condition of the vehicle.

## Frequently asked questions

### How are the cars tested?

All MOT testing stations have approved facilities where statutory testing is carried out, using a range of specialist equipment.

There are standard test procedures laid down and a manual available for reference. You can watch your test being conducted but please do not interrupt the tester.

All MOT testers have been trained by VI and their competence to test is checked regularly. The procedures and standards are laid down in the MOT inspection manual.

fees

### How can I find out how much it will cost?

Ask any vehicle testing station about the current test and retest fees. They are also displayed on the fees and appeals poster in the public area of MOT testing stations.

about VI

### Who supervises the scheme?

The Vehicle Inspectorate (VI) is the government agency responsible for supervising the MOT scheme.



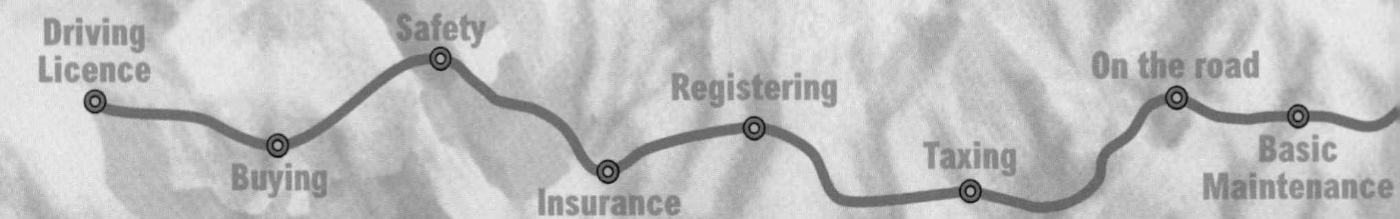

It does this by:

- authorising MOT testing stations and nominated testers
- setting standards for testing and conditions of appointment for the testing stations and testers
- training authorised examiners and MOT testers
- visiting garages on a regular basis and carrying out checks to ensure testing standards are maintained on tester's competence and maintenance of approved equipment
- taking disciplinary action where tests are not being carried out to the required standards
- dealing with appeals and complaints from MOT customers
- conducting roadside emissions checks.

## Where do I take my car for the test?

There are around 19,000 garages authorised as MOT testing stations in Great Britain which can carry out your MOT test. These garages are easily identifiable by the blue three triangles logo which they have to display.

There is a maximum fee for the test which will be displayed on a poster inside the testing station.

## I have just bought a car without an MOT. Can I drive it to the garage?

You may drive it to a prebooked appointment at a testing station. The vehicle must be insured for your use, but does not have to be taxed.

**I bought a second-hand car. When I compared the MOT certificate with one from another car, it seems very flimsy. I think it might be a fake. What should I do?**

Please ring VI's MOT enquiry line on 0845 600 5977. Calls are charged at the local rate.

**I have lost the MOT certificate for my car. Will I need to get it retested?**

A duplicate certificate can be obtained from the MOT testing station which tested your vehicle. If the MOT station is no longer in business, your local VI office may be able to help, provided you have details of where and when your vehicle was tested. The maximum that can be charged for a duplicate certificate is £10.00.

**I have noticed the registration number on the certificate is incorrect. Is it still valid?**

If after having your vehicle tested you find an error on the test certificate, a replacement certificate with the correct details should be obtained from the MOT test station which tested your vehicle.

### When I bought my car last week it had a new test certificate but I have since discovered the brake pipes are corroded. Should it have passed?

You must let VI know as soon as possible. They will then offer an appointment within five working days to recheck your vehicle without charge provided:

- not more than three months has elapsed since the time of the test for a corrosion defect

  or

- up to 28 days for other defects.

appeals

### The garage failed my car for incorrect beam alignment and a fault in the steering. I think they are only after the repair work. What do I do?

You must complete an appeal form (VT17) obtainable from any MOT testing station or VI and return it to one of our offices within 14 working days of the test along with a full test fee. The Vehicle Inspectorate will then offer an appointment within five days to recheck your vehicle. If your appeal is successful some or all of the test fee will be refunded to you. Do not have your car repaired as this may affect the outcome of the appeal.

If you have any complaints or you are unhappy with the way your test was conducted please complain to the Area

Manager at your local VI office. (Their address is displayed on a poster at the testing station). They want to hear about unsatisfactory aspects of performance as these assist them in the monitoring of the MOT scheme.

Local Offices

### How can I get more information about the VI service and performance standards?

You can contact the Area Manager at your local VI office or call 0870 60 60 440. The addresses can be found in chapter 15 and on posters in the testing station, or check out the website.

MOT Test
Going Green
Selling
Further Information
Going Abroad
Breakdowns
Security

chapter ten

# breakdowns

being prepared

if you break down

if you break down on a motorway

frequently asked questions

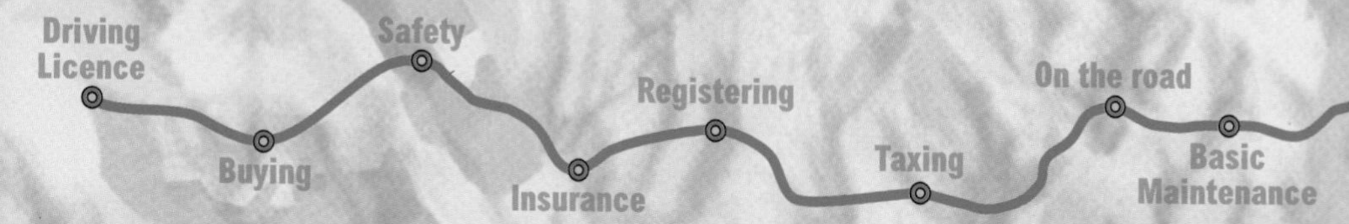

## Being prepared

accident advice

You can reduce the chances of a breakdown with preventive maintenance and regular vehicle checks. However, no matter how careful you are, your vehicle can still break down – a puncture or burst tyre is always possible.

Knowing how to deal with such a situation efficiently and safely is essential knowledge for every driver.

preparation

Many breakdowns are the result of

- neglect
- failing to make routine checks
- inadequate preventive maintenance
- abuse of the vehicle.

Don't drive on ignoring noises or symptoms which are unusual or if you're concerned that the problem might be serious.

Carry a tool kit in your vehicle. The following items are useful to keep for emergencies:

- warning triangle (or other permitted warning device)
- spare bulbs and fuses
- torch
- vinyl tape
- wire
- jump leads

- tow rope
- pliers
- plastic container of water.

## Breakdown organisations

By joining a national organisation or taking out breakdown insurance, you'll save a great deal of time and money if you break down. The annual fee is usually less than the cost of a single motorway breakdown call-out. Most services include an option to take your vehicle and passengers either to your destination or to your home.

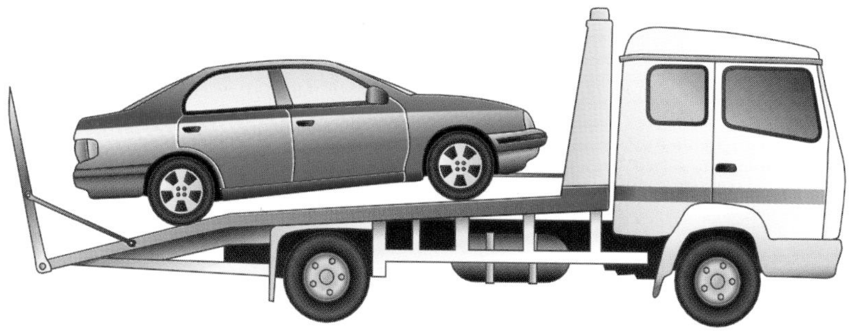

## Warning devices

There are various warning devices that you can buy to place on the road to warn other drivers when you have broken down. Don't use any of these warning devices



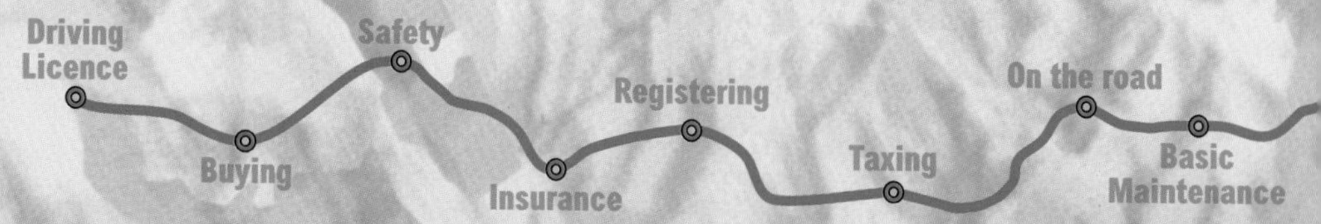

- on a motorway
- as an excuse to leave your car in a dangerous position.

## Advance warning triangles

Advance warning triangles fold flat and don't take up much space in the car. You should carry one and use it to warn other road users if your car is obstructing the highway or is in a dangerous position as a result of a breakdown or an accident. You should place the triangle on the road, well back from the car:

- on a straight level road, put the triangle 45 m (147 ft) from your vehicle
- on a winding or hilly road, put the triangle where drivers will see it before they have to deal with any bend or hump in the road
- on a very narrow road, put the triangle on the nearside verge or footpath.

Always use your hazard warning lights as well as a warning triangle, especially at night. **Do not use a warning triangle on the motorway.**

## Other warning devices

These include traffic cones, flat traffic delineators (which resemble a flattened cone) and traffic pyramids. At least four of any of these should be placed in a line behind your vehicle



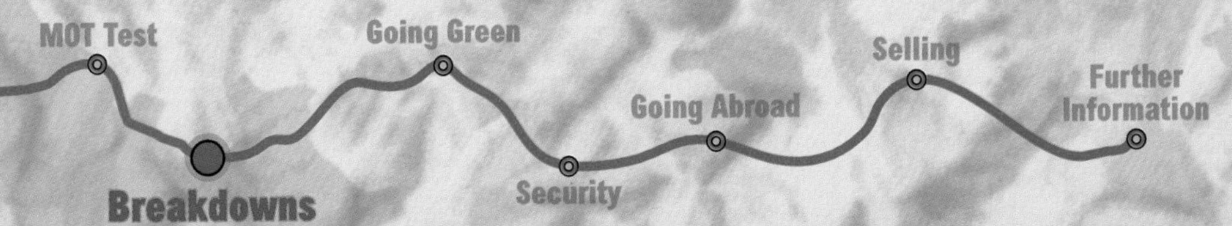

to guide traffic past. **Do not use these on the motorway**. A flashing amber light may be used with any of these warning devices, but may not be used on its own.

Alternatively, a flexible yellow sheet displaying a red triangle can be placed on the vehicle, provided it does not obscure the number plate, lights or reflectors.

Highway Code

## If you break down

As a general rule, brake as gently as possible and pull over as far to the left as possible to keep your vehicle away from approaching traffic.

If the breakdown affects your control of the car:

- try to keep in a straight line by holding the steering wheel firmly
- avoid braking severely
- steer gently on to the side of the road as you lose speed.

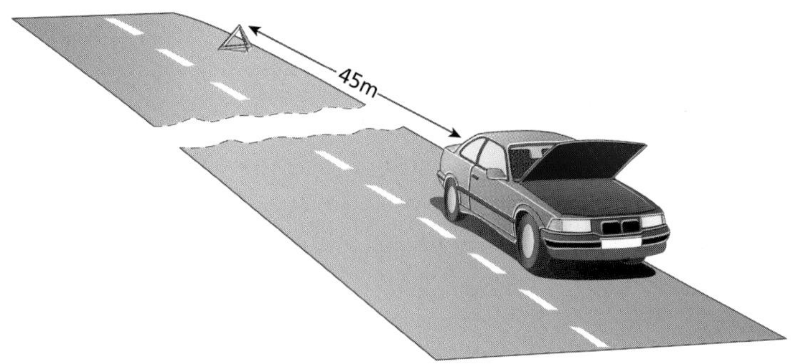




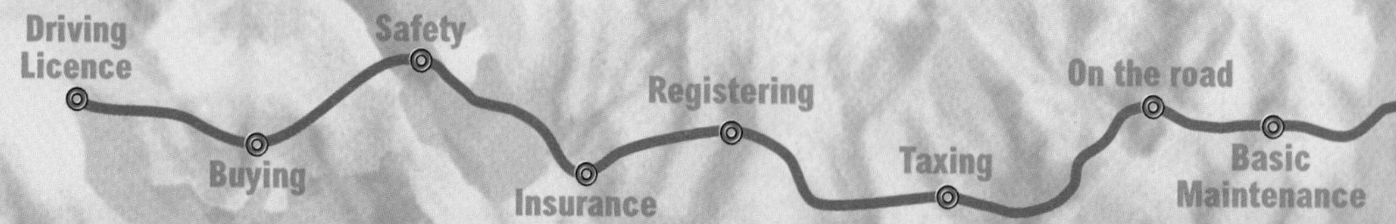

If possible, get your car well off the road and

- use your hazard warning lights to warn others
- keep your sidelights on if it is dark or visibility is poor
- do not stand behind your vehicle where you might obscure the lights. You could also get hit by another vehicle
- use a warning device, particularly if you've broken down near a bend, or over the brow of a hill. Do not use one if you have broken down on a motorway
- keep children and animals under control, and away from the road
- contact the police if your vehicle is causing an obstruction, and a breakdown service if you're unable to rectify the fault yourself.

Don't

- ask for help from passing strangers
- accept help from strangers
- leave your vehicle for any longer than you really have to.

## If you break down on the motorway

Highway Code

If you cannot reach the next exit or service area, steer your vehicle onto the hard shoulder as safely as possible, and as far to the left as you can, away from traffic. When you stop it is a good idea to have your wheels turned to the left, so that if you are hit from behind, your vehicle is not pushed on to the main carriageway.

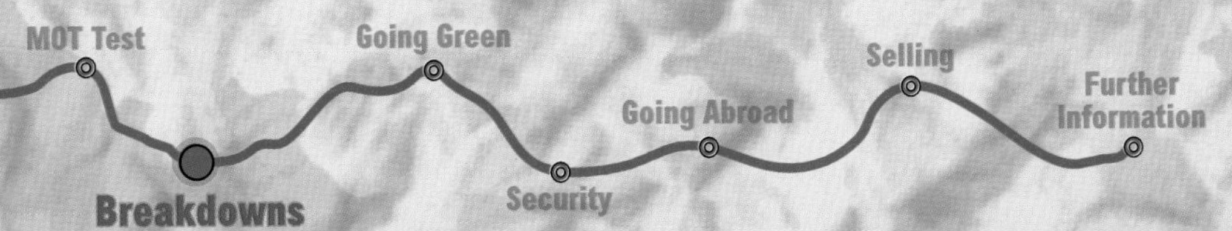

Once you have stopped:

- switch on your hazard lights to warn other drivers you've broken down
- make sure your sidelights are on in poor visibility or at night
- don't open the offside doors (near the traffic flow)
- warn your passengers of the dangers of passing vehicles
- keep animals inside
- with your passengers, leave the vehicle by the nearside door, away from the traffic. Lock all doors, except the front passenger door
- ask your passengers to wait near the vehicle, but on the embankment away from the hard shoulder
- telephone the emergency services. If possible use a roadside emergency telephone which will pinpoint your position, rather than a mobile phone.

Never

- attempt even simple repairs on the motorway
- place any kind of warning device on the carriageway or hard shoulder.

## Disabled drivers

If you have any kind of mobility difficulty you should stay in your vehicle and

- switch on your hazard warning lights
- display a 'Help' pennant or use a mobile phone, if you have one in your vehicle, and be prepared to advise the emergency services of your location.

## Calling for help

Police-controlled emergency telephones are on most stretches of motorway at one mile intervals.

Look for a telephone symbol and arrow on marker posts 100 m (328 ft) apart along the hard shoulder. The arrow directs you to the nearest phone on your side of the carriageway. Walk to the telephone, keeping on the inside of the hard shoulder.

Highway Code

Never cross the carriageway or an exit or entry slip road to reach a phone or for any other purpose.

The emergency phone connects you to police control, who will put you through to a breakdown service. Always face the traffic when you speak on the telephone.

You'll be asked for

- the number on the telephone, which gives your precise location
- details of your vehicle and your membership details, if you belong to one of the motoring organisations
- details of the fault.

If you're a vulnerable motorist such as a woman travelling alone, make this clear to the operator. You'll be told approximately how long you'll have to wait.

Highway Code

### Using a mobile phone

If you are unable to use an emergency telephone, use a mobile phone if you have one in your vehicle. However, before you call, make sure that you can give the police precise details of your location. Marker posts on the side of the hard shoulder identify your location and you should provide these details when you call.

### Waiting for the breakdown truck

Wait on the bank near your vehicle, so you can see the emergency services arriving. Don't wait in your vehicle unless another vehicle pulls up near you, and you feel at risk.

Many motorway deaths are caused by vehicles driving into people on the hard shoulder. When you're on the hard shoulder you're much more likely to be injured by motorway traffic than suffer a personal attack.

If anyone approaches

- get into the vehicle
- lock all the doors



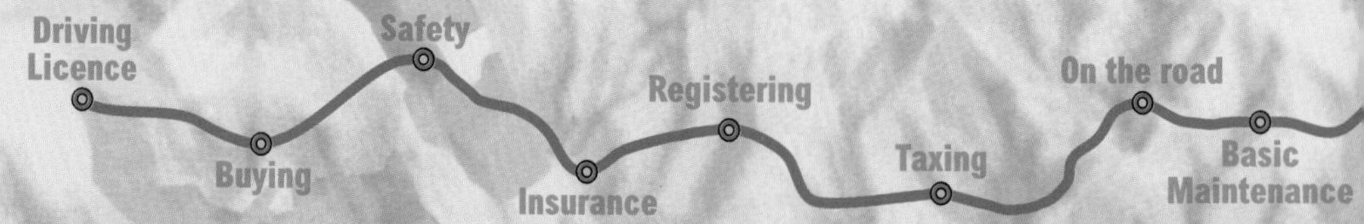

- lower the window slightly
- speak through a small gap.

Then

- ask for identity
- tell them that the police have been told and the emergency services are coming.

A person claiming to be from the emergency services should have

- an identity card
- your details: your name and information about the breakdown.

Leave your vehicle again as soon as you feel the danger has passed.

## Frequently asked questions

### I often travel alone. Are there any precautions I can take?

You should join a breakdown service and if possible carry a mobile phone. You might feel vulnerable if you're travelling alone and you break down, especially on an isolated stretch of road, a dual carriageway or a motorway. You should spend as little time as possible away from your vehicle.



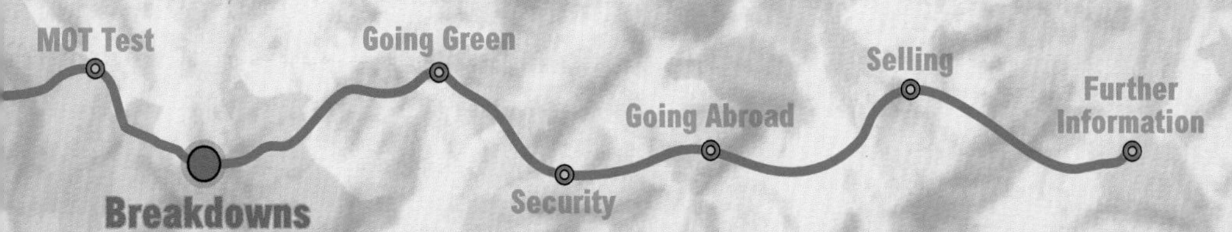

When you telephone for assistance, make it clear to the operator that you're travelling alone. Priority will often be given in these cases.

## Can I tow my friend's vehicle that has broken down?

If the vehicle cannot be repaired where it has broken down, it will need to be moved.

There are three options:

- being recovered by a breakdown organisation you belong to (the best)
- calling out a local garage (probably the most costly)
- being towed by a friend (the most dangerous – should in no circumstances be considered by an inexperienced driver).

## What if I can't get on to the hard shoulder on a motorway?

Switch on your hazard warning lights and leave your vehicle only when you can safely get clear of the carriageway.

## How can I rejoin the motorway from a stationary position?

This can be dangerous, use the hard shoulder to build up speed before joining the other traffic when it's safe to do so.



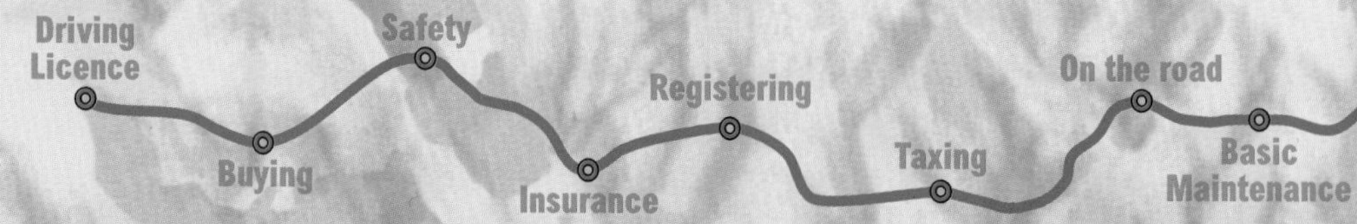

Don't try to move out from behind another vehicle or force your way into the stream of traffic.

Remember to switch off your hazard warning lights before moving off.

## If I break down on a dual carriageway is the procedure the same as for a motorway?

Some dual carriageways are similar to motorways; they have

- a hard shoulder to pull on to
- emergency telephones at regular intervals.

However, most dual carriageways do not have a wide hard shoulder. If you break down on one of these

- get your car safely away from the road, if you can – onto the grass verge or lay-by if there is one. Take care if there's long grass which could ignite from the heat of a catalytic converter
- use your hazard warning lights and warning triangle or other warning device to warn others
- go to the nearest telephone and arrange assistance
- keep animals safely in the car.



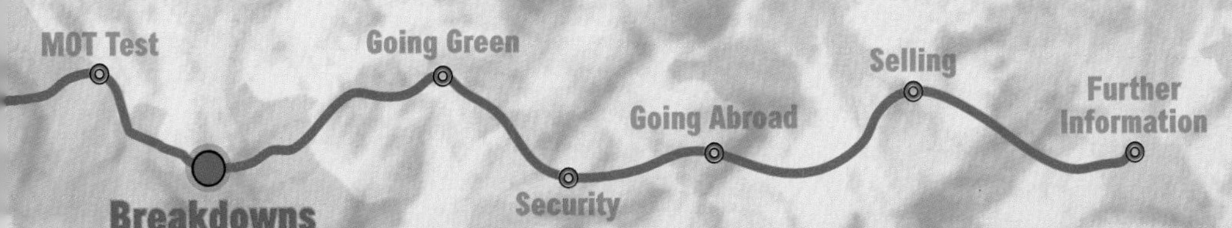

### What if I have a puncture?

If your car suddenly becomes unstable or you begin to feel steering problems, you might have a puncture or a blow-out (burst tyre).

If you have a puncture:

- try not to panic
- take your foot off the accelerator
- don't brake suddenly
- try to keep a straight course by holding the steering wheel firmly
- stop gradually at the side of the road
- get the vehicle away from the traffic (onto the hard shoulder if you're on a motorway).

If you have to move the vehicle, do so very slowly to avoid further damage to the tyre or wheel rim. Get the vehicle to a place of safety before attempting to change the wheel.

If you can't get off the road altogether, use your warning triangle, or any other permitted warning device, particularly if you're near a bend, to warn other drivers. Never use one on a motorway.

If necessary, wait for assistance.

Remember:

- secure the vehicle when changing any wheel by applying the handbrake and using chocks if available.
- always try to work on a level surface.
- retighten wheel nuts/studs after changing a wheel.

# chapter eleven

# going green

environmental consequences

exhaust emissions

what you can do to help

traffic management

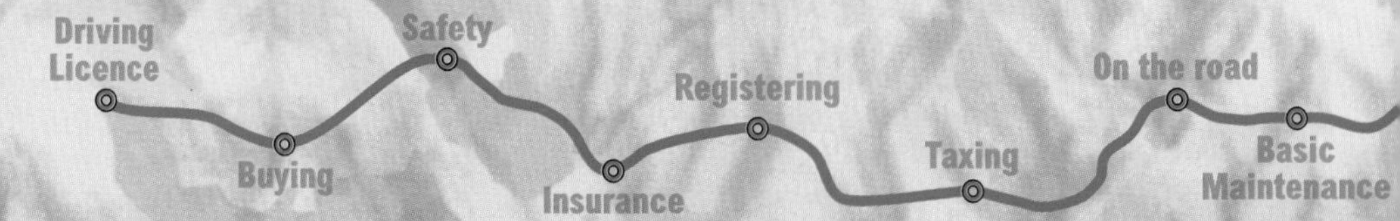

## Environmental consequences

Transport is an essential part of modern life, but we cannot ignore its environmental consequences – local, regional and global.

doing your bit

There's increasing public concern for the protection of our environment, with the result that many motor vehicle manufacturers are devoting more time, effort and resources to the development of environmentally friendly vehicles. Considerable research and effort is taking place to develop lighter, smaller and more efficient vehicles for town use. Much of that effort has concentrated on developing electrically powered vehicles with the ability to operate for longer periods before recharging.

travelwise

Considerable research and effort is taking place to develop more fuel efficient vehicles. This includes steps to reduce vehicle weight, increase engine efficiency and introduce alternative fuel and engine technologies. Emissions of local pollutants from new road vehicles have been greatly reduced over the last decade, in response to successively tighter mandatory emissions standards, by a variety of technologies including the use of catalytic converters on petrol-engined cars.

### The effects of pollution

air quality

Motor vehicles account for most of the movement of people and goods. The increased number of vehicles on the roads has damaged the environment; it has resulted in

- changes to the landscape
- air pollution, causing
  - human health problems, in particular respiratory disease
  - damage to vegetation
- building deterioration
- bridge weakening
- changes to communities
- depletion of natural resources
- disruption of wildlife.

atmosphere

Fuel combustion produces carbon dioxide ($CO_2$) , a major greenhouse gas, and transport accounts for about one-fifth of the carbon dioxide we produce in this country.

## Exhaust emissions

MOT tests now include a strict exhaust emission test to ensure that cars are properly tuned. This means they operate more efficiently and cause less air pollution.

emissions

### Petrol engines

The modern petrol engine has been designed to operate more efficiently to meet increasingly stringent emissions standards. Fuel injection, electronic engine management systems and redesigned exhaust systems are key factors in this improvement in reducing exhaust pollution.

Ever stricter controls on exhaust emissions require catalytic converters to be fitted to the exhaust system of all new petrol-engined vehicles. Ultra-low sulphur petrol is also now widely available for petrol vehicles. The lower sulphur content in this fuel reduces exhaust production further.

### Catalytic converters

Catalytic converters are exhaust treatment systems which remove up to 90 per cent of carbon monoxide, nitrogen oxide and hydrocarbons.

The converter has a honeycomb structure with a total surface area about equal to a football pitch. This surface is coated with a 'washcoat' containing particles of precious

metals such as platinum, palladium and rhodium. These promote chemical reactions of gases in the exhaust, converting harmful pollutant gases to harmless water vapour, nitrogen and carbon dioxide.

The oxygen content of the exhaust is monitored and a sensor triggers controls to adjust the air–fuel ratio. The converter only deals with toxic and polluting gases. Carbon dioxide is still produced.

Leaded petrol cannot be used in vehicles fitted with a catalytic converter. Even one tankful can permanently damage the system.

### Diesel engines

These engines are very efficient and produce less carbon dioxide (a global warming gas) than spark ignition (petrol and LPG fuelled) engines. Compared with petrol-engined cars they also emit less carbon monoxide and hydrocarbons. They do, however, produce more emissions of oxides of nitrogen (NOx) and particulates, which are bad for local air quality.

Newer vehicles have to meet strict new emissions standards aimed at reducing these pollutants, and all diesel vehicles now use ultra-low sulphur diesel which reduces exhaust pollution.



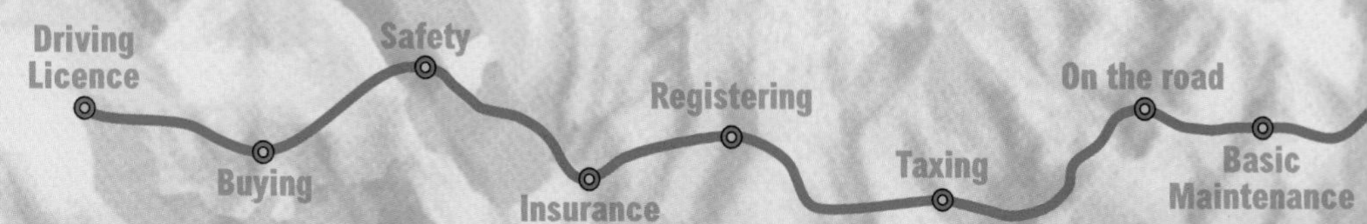

### Alternative fuels and technologies

Powershift

A number of vehicles running on more environmentally friendly alternative fuels and technologies are now available. Vehicles powered by Liquid Petroleum Gas (LPG) are now widely available and the number of LPG refuelling sites is increasing steadily. LPG is cheaper to use than petrol or diesel and produces fewer emissions of air pollutants. However, LPG does produce more carbon dioxide than diesel. Other vehicles running on alternative fuels and technologies currently available include battery electric vehicles, which produce no tailpipe pollution, and hybrid electric vehicles, which combine an electric motor with a conventional petrol or diesel engine. Hybrid electric vehicles can be very clean and fuel efficient.

The Powershift programme offers grants to purchasers of vehicles powered by alternative fuels and technologies offering environmental benefits or conversion of existing petrol or diesel vehicles (of less than one year old). The Powershift hotline can be contacted on 0845 6021425.

## What you can do to help

### Use your car only when it is necessary:

- avoid using your car for very short journeys, especially when the engine is cold – walk or cycle instead

- use public transport when you can
- if you need to travel by car, consider sharing with a colleague or friend who is making the same journey (for example, to work or the 'school run')
- plan your journey beforehand and try to use uncongested routes
- avoid using your car when air pollution is high. Information about air pollution is available on
  - Ceefax (page 410) or Teletext
  - Air Pollution Information Service – Freephone 0800 556677
  - local radio or newspapers
  - this book's own website

## Keep your vehicle well maintained:

- make sure the engine is in tune. Badly tuned cars and vans use more fuel and emit more exhaust fumes. Most badly polluting vehicles can be retuned by a garage within 15 minutes and at a low cost
- have your vehicle serviced as recommended by the manufacturer. The cost of a service may well be less than the cost of running a badly maintained vehicle. Make sure your garage includes an emissions check in the service
- make sure that your tyres are properly inflated. Incorrect tyre pressure results in shorter tyre life and may create a danger. In addition, under-inflation causes increased fuel consumption and emissions
- if you do your own maintenance, make sure that you send oil, old batteries and used tyres to a garage or local authority site for recycling or safe disposal. Don't pour oil down the drain. It's illegal, harmful to the environment and could lead to prosecution.

oil care code

risk profile

## Drive more efficiently:

- if you need to use the choke to start the engine when it is cold, push it in as soon as the engine will run smoothly without it. Drive off as soon as possible after starting
- switch the engine off if you are likely to be stuck in traffic for longer than two minutes or if you are parked
- drive sensibly and always keep within the speed limit. Good driving habits save fuel
- as soon as traffic conditions allow, use the highest appropriate gear and avoid over-revving

- wherever possible avoid rapid acceleration or heavy braking as this leads to greater fuel consumption and more pollution. Driving smoothly can reduce fuel consumption by about 15 per cent as well as reducing wear and tear on your vehicle
- slow down. Vehicles travelling at 70 mph use up to 30 per cent more fuel to cover the same distance as those travelling at 50 mph
- check your fuel consumption regularly to make sure you are getting the most from your car
- save fuel by not carrying unnecessary weight in your car. If your car's roof rack is removable, take it off when it's not in use to reduce wind resistance
- use air conditioning sparingly – running air conditioning continuously increases fuel consumption by about 15 per cent.

**Select for economy and low emissions:**

- when buying a new vehicle choose a fuel-efficient model. For the fuel consumption of new vehicles, check out the website
- cars with automatic transmission use about 10 per cent more fuel than similar models with manual transmission
- use unleaded petrol. Consult your dealer or garage to check if your vehicle can use unleaded petrol and, if necessary, have the engine adjusted to use it
- consider using ultra-low sulphur petrol which is becoming more widely available at filling stations
- when replacing tyres, consider buying energy saving types which have reduced rolling resistance. These increase fuel efficiency



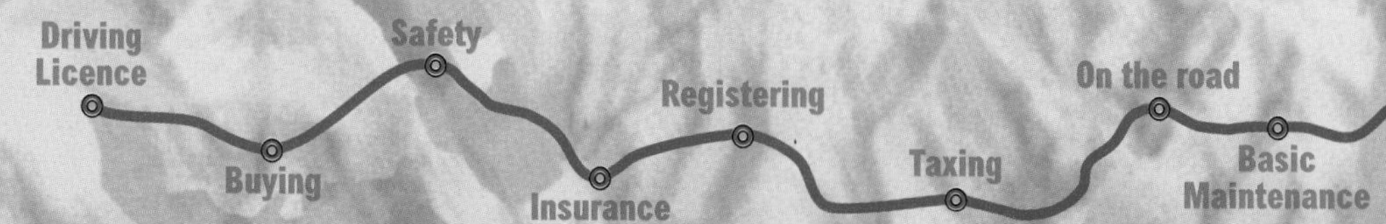

- be aware that the use of electrical devices increases fuel consumption.

### Off-road activities

Whatever type of vehicle you drive, if you take part in off-road activities, remember

- avoid damaging walls, fences, paths, grassland, etc.
- take care not to harm livestock or wildlife
- respect the countryside in general – follow the Country Code
- drive in a responsible manner at all times.

## Traffic management

Continuous research has resulted in new methods of helping the environment by easing traffic flow. All drivers need to be aware of the restrictions that apply and should consider using alternative transport. Use public transport whenever you can.

### Traffic flow

Highway Code

The strict parking rules in major cities and towns help the traffic flow. The 'red routes' in London are an example of this and have cut journey times and improved traffic flow considerably.



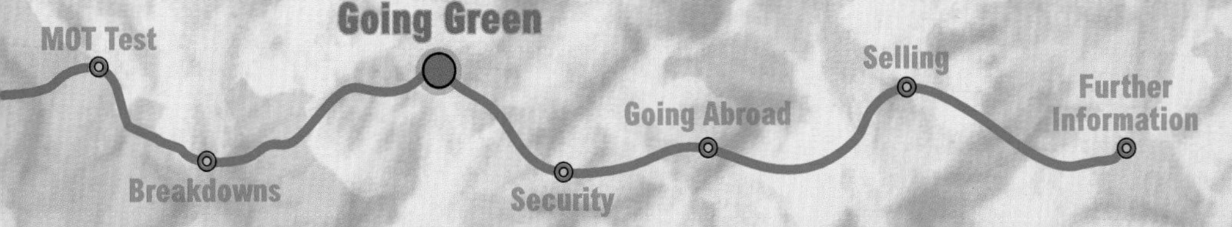

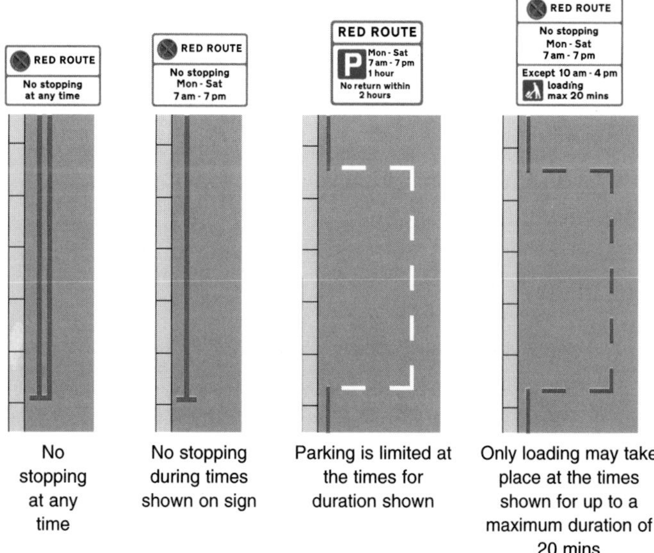


No stopping at any time

No stopping during times shown on sign

Parking is limited at the times for duration shown

Only loading may take place at the times shown for up to a maximum duration of 20 mins

## Speed reduction

Traffic calming measures, including road humps and chicanes, help to keep vehicle speeds low in sensitive areas. There are also an increasing number of areas where a 20 mph speed limit is in force. Pedestrians are much more likely to survive an accident with a motor vehicle travelling at 20 mph than at 40 mph. These areas, where traffic is moving more slowly, are usually safer for cyclists as well.



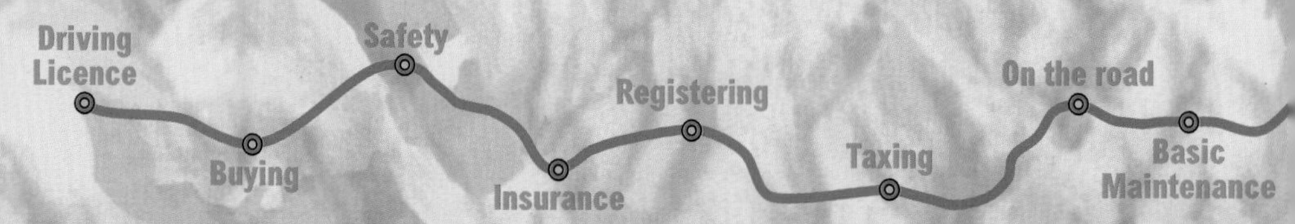

For further information contact:

**Public Enquiry Unit**
**Department of the Environment, Transport and the Regions**
Eland House
Bressenden Place
London SW1E 5DU
Tel: 020 7890 3000

**Environmental Transport Association**
10 Church Street
Weybridge
Surrey
KT13 8RS
Tel: 01932 828882
Fax: 01932 829015

emissions

New Car Fuel Consumption Emissions Figure booklet can be obtained from:
**Vehicle Certification Agency**
1 The Eastgate Office Centre
Eastgate Road
Bristol BS5 6XX

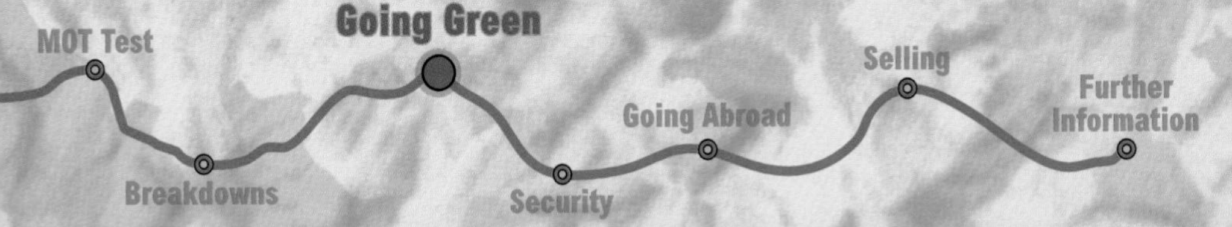

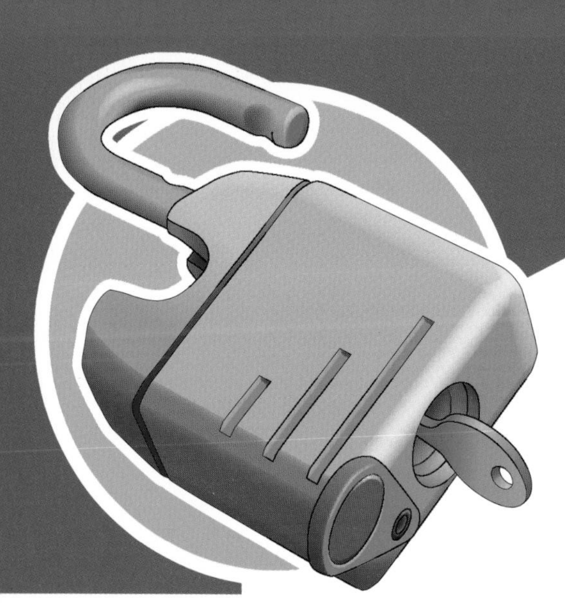

chapter twelve

# car security

preventing theft

security devices

parking

useful contacts

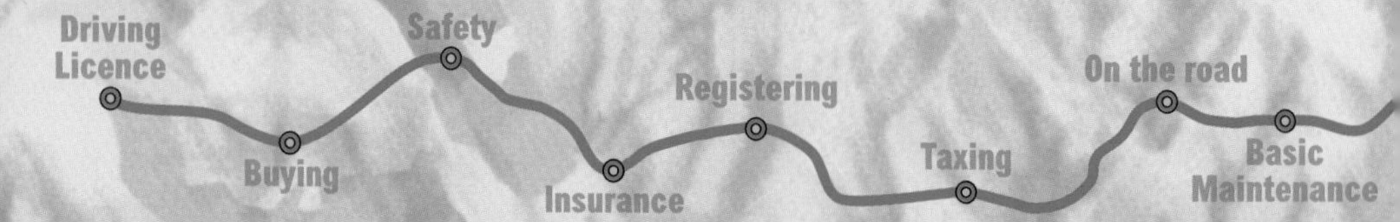

## Preventing theft

statistics

Over a quarter of all recorded crimes are car thefts or thefts from cars - like stereos and mobile phones. It's a problem that affects us all no matter where we live. It diverts much police time and can have serious and sometimes fatal consequences.

The thieves vary from the opportunists to the professionals who often work in gangs and target specific models for which they already have a buyer, sometimes in another country. Even more common are thefts from private cars. Once more the culprits range from the opportunists, who snatch valuables from unlocked cars, to the professionals, who comb whole areas and steal car radios from poorly secured vehicles.

most at risk

Having your vehicle stolen or broken into is at best an inconvenience and at worst very distressing. While determined thieves would probably be able to steal or get into any vehicle, they are usually too busy with the poorly secured ones. If your vehicle is secured, and preferably alarmed and immobilised, they may well leave it alone.

Security is also very much in the minds of car buyers since the battle against car crime has yet to be won. In 1998, police forces in England and Wales recorded over a million offences – just over one third of these involved the theft of a vehicle, while the remainder involved theft from a vehicle.



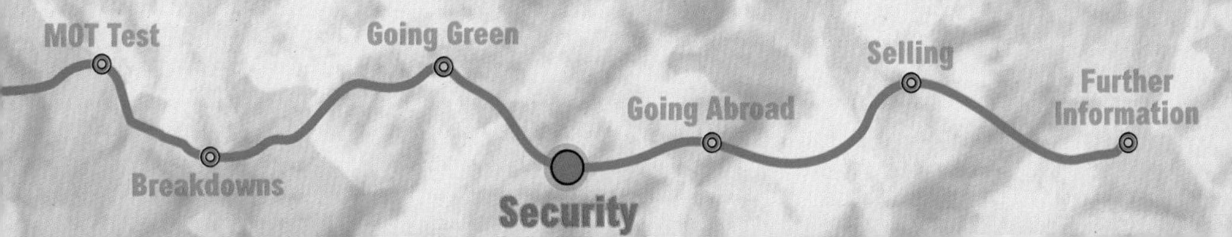

It is widely accepted that the theft of vehicle contents goes largely unreported, and the Home Office's British Crime Survey suggests that the actual figure is up to four times the reported figure. The government have since announced a target to reduce the number of thefts of, and from, vehicles by 30 per cent over the five years ending in March 2004.

Taking a vehicle without the owner's consent, or with the intention of driving it recklessly, is a criminal offence. Such actions sometimes end in death, usually for other, innocent road users.

crime reduction

To make it more difficult for the would-be thief, particularly the opportunist, there are some precautions you can take to secure your vehicle:

- fit an anti-theft device (alarm and/or immobiliser)
- use a visible security device (to lock steering wheel, handbrake, etc.)
- have the vehicle registration number etched on all windows.

## Risk of theft

Periodically the Home Office produces a publication called the Car Theft Index. Based on details of reported thefts in the last year, which are held on the Police National Computer, this booklet gives an indication about the risk of theft for practically every type of car on the road. The risk is shown



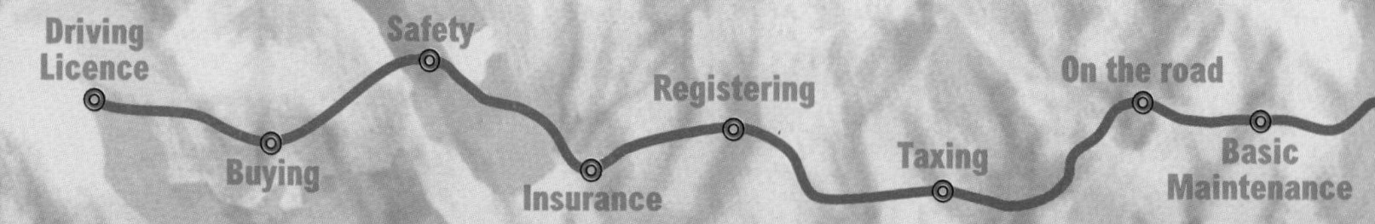

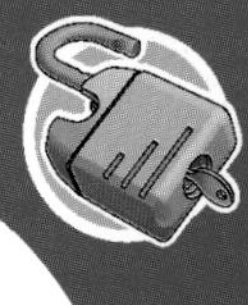

for the vehicle type and year of registration by a colour code representing 'lower risk', 'medium risk' and 'higher risk'. All owners of high risk cars, especially, are urged to improve the security of their vehicles either through fitting an immobiliser, or, perhaps, where the value of the car makes this prohibitive, to use an effective mechanical immobiliser, like an approved steering wheel lock.

most at risk

The Car Theft Index is available free of charge from your local Crime Prevention Officer, or from the Home Office either on their website or by faxing a request to the Home Office Communications Directorate on 020 7273 2568.

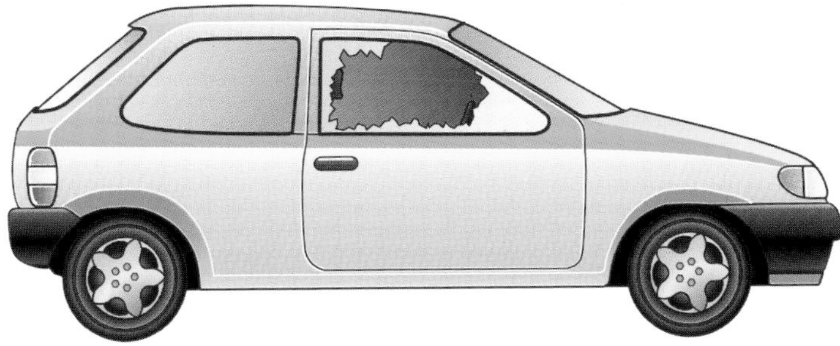

### Vehicle Watch

most at risk

Join a Vehicle Watch scheme, if there is one in your area.

This scheme reduces the risk of having your car stolen by displaying high visibility stickers on the front and rear windscreens of your vehicle. There are two types of stickers:

- vehicle watch – by displaying these you are inviting the police to stop your vehicle if they see it in use between midnight and 5am
- 25 plus - by displaying these you are also inviting them to stop your vehicle at any time of the day if it is being driven by anyone apparently under 25 years of age.

Stickers and additional information about the scheme can be obtained from the Crime Prevention Officer at your local police station.

### The Hyena campaign

The Hyena campaign has a long-term objective of making car crime as socially unacceptable as drinking and driving. It is vital that everyone works together to reduce the opportunities for the car criminal.

## Security devices

The door and steering locks fitted to most cars cannot be relied upon to deter a thief. A wide array of other security



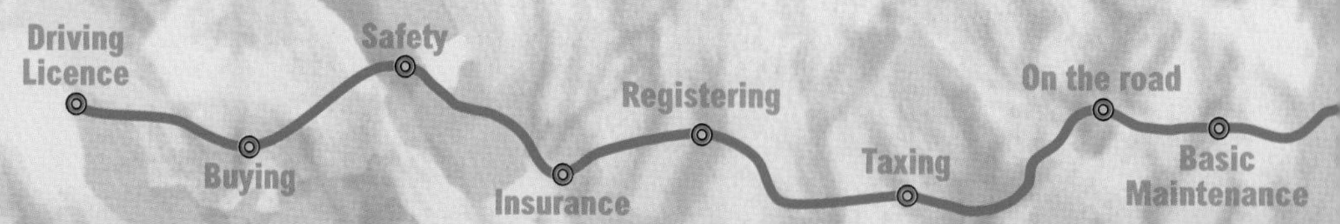

devices such as alarm systems and immobilisers are available, either as original or aftermarket equipment. These devices can substantially improve the security of your vehicle.

*What Car?* magazine, *Auto Express* magazine and Thatcham (the Motor Insurance Repair Research Centre) all test vehicles and security devices and publish the results. Electronic immobilisers and alarm systems that have been tested and proved to offer a significant level of security may attract insurance discounts, provided that they are fitted by an installer approved by the Vehicle Security Installation Board (VSIB). Details of these organisations can be found on the website. Lists of security products and approved installers can be obtained from your local Crime Prevention Officer or direct from the organisations themselves. Speak to your insurer for information about discounts when fitting security devices.

## Locks

In most thefts from closed vehicles, and in nearly all thefts of vehicles, it is necessary for the thief to get into the car. Entry is usually gained through a door, a window or the luggage compartment. Door locks which conform to British Standard (BS) AU 209 Part 1A: 1992 give a good level of basic security. They will prevent the door being easily forced open and the internal latch mechanism being manipulated with a simple device such as a coat hanger.

### Central locking

Central locking systems which conform to BS AU 209 Part 5b:1996 include locks which meet the requirements of Part 1A and ensure that all the doors and luggage compartments lock when the driver's door is locked. This should reduce the risk of any door being left unlocked. Such systems are especially convenient if you often carry passengers and need to ensure that their doors are locked as well.

### Deadlocks

In recent years many cars have been fitted with deadlocks (sometimes called 'double locks' or 'super locks'). The effect of these is that even if a thief breaks a window the door cannot be unlocked using the interior controls. Such cars are less attractive to opportunist thieves as they usually have to climb in and out through a broken window. Deadlocking systems can be approved to BS AU 209 Part 6a: 1996.

### Immobilisers

For many years, new cars have had to be fitted with a device to prevent unauthorised use. This is usually in the form of a steering column lock combined with an ignition switch. These operate when the key is removed, although the steering wheel should be turned until a click is heard to engage the column lock, as this makes it harder for the thief to get round the systems.



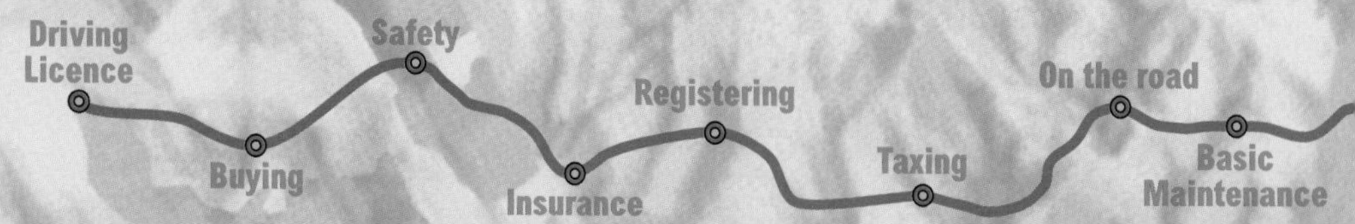

All new mass produced passenger cars designed after 31 December 1996, or built after 30 September 1998, will be fitted with an electronic immobiliser. This is a device designed to prevent a vehicle being driven away powered by its own engine. Some earlier cars will also be fitted with an electronic immobiliser, but as these are not usually visible, first check the manufacturer's specifications.

If your car does not have an electronic immobiliser already fitted, it can be made more secure by having an aftermarket device installed or by using an additional mechanical immobiliser.

## Additional mechanical immobilisers

These devices generally have a strong locking mechanism and prevent the use of one or more essential controls. Early versions connected the brake pedal to the steering wheel. Many recent models lock a bar to the steering wheel, preventing it from being rotated. Some are specifically designed to prevent the removal of an airbag. Others lock the gear lever in a fixed position or connect the handbrake to the gear lever. These are not suitable for cars with a screwed-in gear lever which can be unscrewed and reinserted free of the immobiliser. Buyers should check when choosing a mechanical immobiliser that it can be stored safely before driving away. The effectiveness of these devices vary greatly and buyers are advised to consult the test reports in the motor magazines before purchasing.

### Aftermarket (electronic) immobilisers

These devices vary from simple ones, that only break the starter motor circuit and can easily be bypassed, to more complex and effective ones which interact with the ignition system to prevent the engine being started. Immobilisers which can be set or come into effect when the engine is running or the vehicle is moving are dangerous, of dubious legality and should be avoided. Thatcham inspect and test immobilisers and publish a list of products that meet their criteria – these will be of proven quality and are unlikely to suffer from erroneous operation. Insurance discounts may be available, but generally are only for passive systems fitted as standard or by an approved installer.



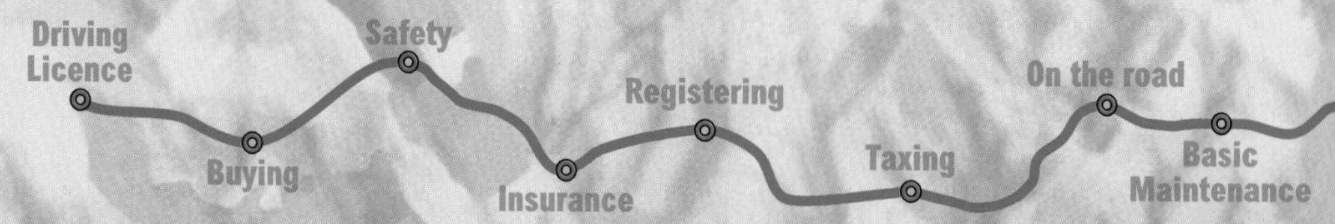

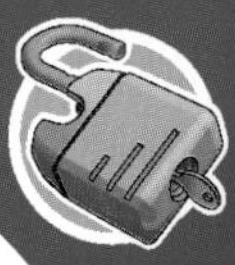

## Alarm systems

An alarm which sounds if a door lock is forced or a window broken can be an effective deterrent.

Alarm systems should only sound following an 'attack' on the vehicle. Local authorities now have legal powers to prosecute the owners of vehicles whose systems give false alarms and cause a nuisance; they can even silence the alarm.

Thatcham (see 'Security devices' section above) inspect and test alarm systems and publish a list of the products meeting their test criteria; these will be of good quality and are unlikely to suffer from false alarms. Insurance discounts may be available, but generally only for passive systems (i.e. systems which arm themselves automatically) fitted as standard or by an approved installer.

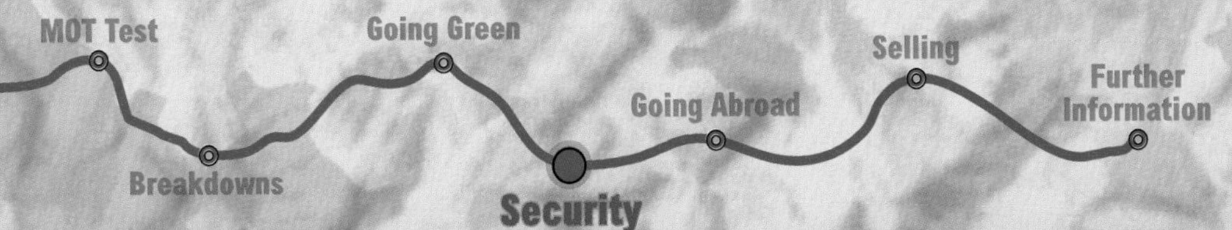

## Tracking and recovery systems

For cars of high value or at high risk of being stolen it might be worth considering an electronic tracking system which helps the police to recover the car if it is stolen. A very determined thief may be able to bypass an immobiliser or simply use a truck to carry the vehicle to a workshop. Cars stolen in this way are difficult to recover. A tracking system will direct the police to where the car is hidden and, although it will not prevent it being stolen, it will greatly improve the chance of it being recovered. Such systems are relatively expensive, and the cost has to be considered in relation to the value of the car in question. Also it cannot be assumed that the police will necessarily have the time or resources to devote to responding to information supplied by these systems.

## Security marking

A cheap method of discouraging car thieves is to have the registration number, VIN or some other unique number etched on all glass surfaces. This will not deter a joy rider, but will make it difficult for a thief to sell the car as a different one with only a change of number plates. Some vehicle manufacturers are now fitting a visible VIN on an inaccessible part of the dashboard. This allows the authenticity of a vehicle identity to be checked without having to gain access to the inside.



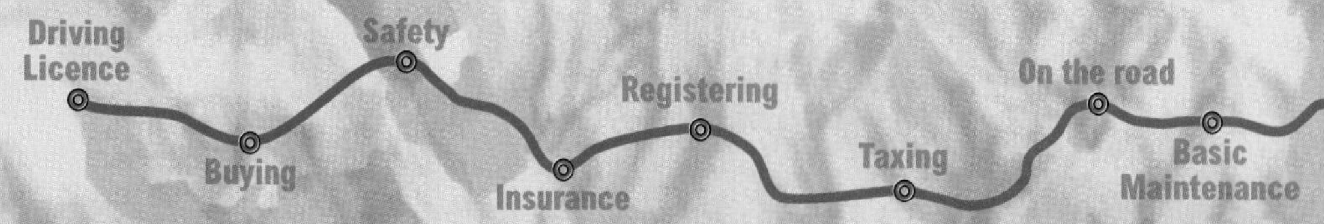

Before using the VIN as a security marking, you must make sure that the manufacturer has a screening process in place for the supply of replacement keys. Otherwise, unauthorised people could obtain keys for your car simply by quoting the VIN number.

Further inexpensive deterrents to theft and aids to recovery are available through the use of 'covert marking'. This is currently commercially available in the form of either microdots, passive transducers or chemically coded solutions. If using a covert system, it is of great importance to advertise its use with the appropriate warning labels supplied by the manufacturers. Most covert systems can be fitted by a vehicle owner, but a fitting service is usually available through a dealer or through a Vehicle Security Installation Board approved installer at a modest extra cost.

## Security Glazing

Certain manufacturers of luxury cars are now offering impact resistant side glazing either as a standard feature or as an optional extra. Vehicles with impact resistant side and rear glazing make it much more difficult for thieves: they keep thieves at bay for far longer than vehicles without such glazing.

This type of side glazing also offers other benefits. It can reduce interior noise levels, reduce the energy consumed by air conditioning systems and, in some cases, reduce weight.

More importantly, security glazing can prevent full or partial ejection in an accident and thus reduce the severity of injuries sustained by the driver or passengers.

There may be a slight increased risk after an accident, either from contact with damaged glass or the glazing preventing easy access. However, compared with partial ejection, this risk is minor.

## Parking

The security features described above offer no absolute guarantee against car theft. To reduce the risks of becoming a victim even further consider the following advice:

Thieves target car parks. Around a quarter of all recorded car crime happens in car parks. When parking in a public car park look for one that is well supervised, with restricted entry and exit points, good lighting and security cameras. Avoid dark corners.

Avoid leaving your vehicle unattended in poorly lit areas, which are known to be a high risk.

Whenever possible

- use attended and Secured Car Parks
- at night, park in a well lit, open location
- if you have a garage, use it and remember to lock it.

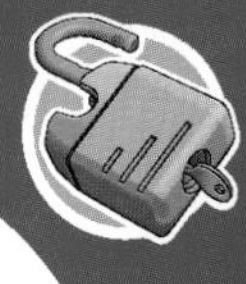

When you leave your vehicle

- lock it
- remove the key
- engage the steering lock
- set the alarm or anti-theft device, if you have one
- close all windows completely (but don't leave pets in a vehicle with the windows completely closed)
- remove all valuables – one in five credit card thefts are from vehicles
- never leave the vehicle documents inside.

## Secured Car Parks scheme

secure car parks

This is a scheme operated by the police. It aims to make car parks safer by setting high standards of internal design, layout and management to discourage crime. Car parks meeting the required standard are entitled to display the official sign for 'Secured Car Parks'. The Crime Prevention Officer at your local police station will be able to advise you of those in your area. Alternatively contact the AA who are scheme administrators on 01256 492733, or check out the website.

## Stereos

Car stereos are one of the prime targets for thieves. Install a security-coded radio. This can deter thieves since the radio is likely to be of little use once removed from the vehicle. Some manufacturers provide security coding for radios supplied in new vehicles.

Another alternative is to install a removable radio. One of these looks exactly like any other radio, but it slides out of its housing. You can lock it away in the boot or take it with you. When parking put the aerial down, if you can, to stop it being vandalised.

## Soft-top vehicles

Never leave a cabriolet or soft-top vehicle where it will obviously be vulnerable.

## Remember: lock it or lose it!

Lock the doors, windows, boot and sun roof every time you leave your car – however briefly.

Take the ignition key out even when the car is parked on your drive or in your garage. Always set the alarm and/or immobiliser, if you have one. Make it so routine that you do it even when filling up with petrol or just popping into the newsagent.

Don't leave valuables on display. That old coat on the back seat may be worthless, but a thief won't know that. He may break in to see if you have left money or credit cards in the pocket.



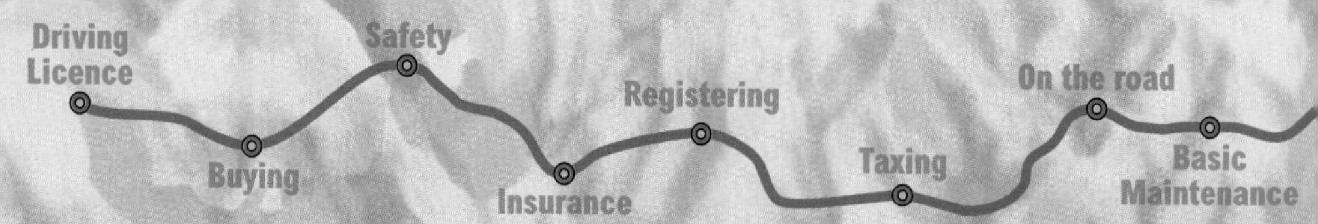

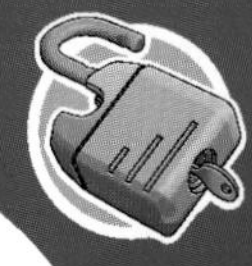

The cost of replacing a broken window is often far more than the value of goods stolen. If you can, take your belongings with you. If you can't, lock everything out of sight in the boot; preferably before you start your journey. If you have to put things in the boot while you are out, make sure nobody is loitering nearby watching you.

In particular, never leave the following anywhere in your car:

- cheque, credit and debit cards – around 150 plastic cards are stolen every day from vehicles
- driving documents and personal correspondence – they could help a thief to sell your car or provide a cover story if stopped by the police
- Mobile phones – 40 per cent of car break-ins involve the theft of a mobile phone. Mark your phone and battery with your postcode and keep a note of its serial number in a safe place. This will help the police to return your phone if it is stolen and subsequently recovered. The Crime Prevention Officer at your local police station or local dealer should be able to provide further information about marking schemes.

Always make sure that your ignition keys are kept in a safe place at all times. Never leave them on hooks, tables or work surfaces in the house. Thieves regularly use fishing rods, magnets and other instruments to reach through letter boxes and windows to steal keys.

## Useful contacts

**Crime Prevention Officers**
Ask for the Crime Prevention Officer at your local police station.

**Crimestoppers**
Tel: 0800 555111

**Vehicle Security Installation Board**
Bates Business Centre
Church Road
Harold Wood
Romford
Essex
RM3 0JF
Tel: 01708 340911

**What Car?**
Haymarket Publications Ltd
60 Waldegrave Road
Teddington
Middlesex
TW11 8LG
Tel: 020 8943 5040

**Auto Express**
Dennis Publishing Ltd
9 Bolsover Street
London
W1P 7HJ
Tel: 020 7917 5558



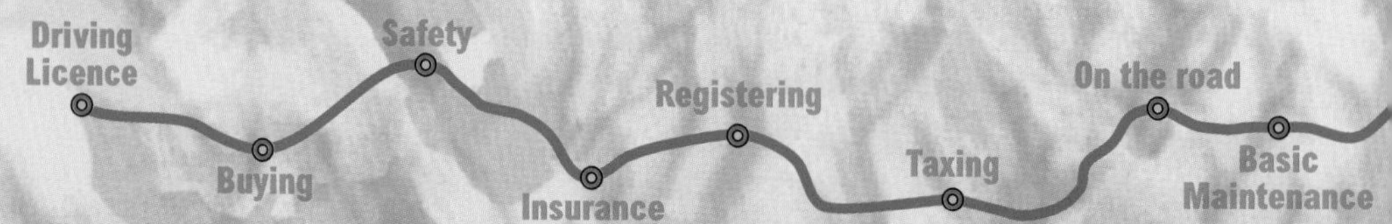

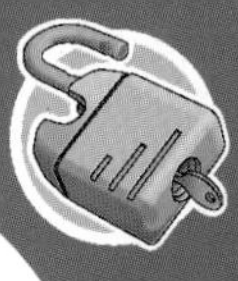

**Home Office**
Vehicle Crime Reduction Section
50 Queen Anne's Gate
London
SW1H 9AT
Tel: 020 7273 3351

**Motor Industry Repair Research Centre**
Calthrop Lane
Thatcham
Berkshire
RG19 4NP
Tel: 01635 868855

(For information about Thatcham)
**Association of British Insurers**
51 Gresham Street
LONDON
EC2V 7HQ
Tel: 020 7600 3333

Details of other organisations and groups can be found in the Autocrime Directory (ISBN 0 9528272 2 0) which is produced by:

**The Thames Valley Partnership**
Old Police Station
Chinnor Road
Thame
Oxfordshire
Tel: 01844 212274

# chapter thirteen

# going abroad

planning your journey

your vehicle

travel checklist

going abroad for more than twelve months

frequently asked questions

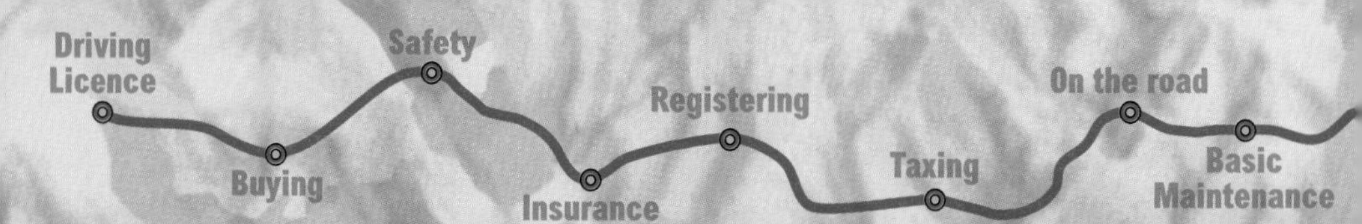

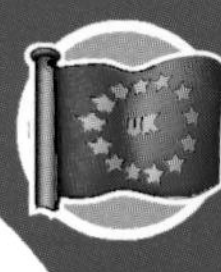


## Planning your journey

Euro route planning

An extensive motorway network runs through most of Europe and there are regular ferry links from many UK ports. There is plenty of opportunity to choose routes which take you closer to your European destination. The Channel Tunnel provides yet another link to continental Europe.

Many East European countries have now opened up their borders, so there's even more of Europe to explore.

world route planning

motoring organisations

If you're planning to take your car abroad, the major motoring organisations can help you to organise and plan the details of your trip. They can

- save you time and money
- set up medical, travel and vehicle insurance
- provide equipment for minor repairs and breakdowns
- help you organise the correct documents for your car, trailer or caravan.

You can often make your trip much easier by using their facilities and experience.

### Your route

road works

Prepare yourself by planning your route in good time.

Again, the motoring organisations can simplify this for you with

- computerised route guides
- summaries of motoring regulations
- details of tolls, etc.

world weather

They will recommend routes from continental ports or airports to specific destinations, using motorways for speed and convenience or scenic routes for pleasure.

## Security

Don't leave handbags, wallets or other attractive items within obvious view inside the vehicle, even when you're inside.



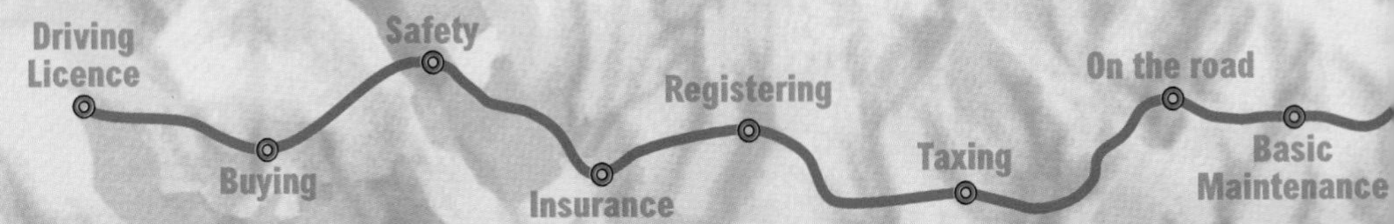

Never leave valuables in an unattended parked vehicle overnight. Loss of possessions, passports, tickets, cash and credit cards can be distressing and inconvenient when you're abroad. Be on your guard against confidence tricksters.

## Your vehicle

Before you travel abroad, have your car thoroughly checked and serviced. Checks to make include

- the spare tyre; make sure it's in good condition
- your tool kit and jack; make sure all items are complete and in working order
- make sure you have your spare car keys.

### Lights

Your lights will need to be altered for driving on the right:

- masks or beam deflectors are required in most countries. These prevent your dipped beam dazzling drivers approaching on the left
- yellow-tinted headlights are no longer required in most countries
- carry a set of replacement bulbs.

### Your mirrors

Check your mirrors: you must have clear all-round vision.

You will need to have exterior rear-view mirrors, especially on the left, for driving on the right hand side of the road.

If you're towing a caravan or trailer, make sure you can see clearly behind, down both sides.

### Seat belts

Check seat belts and child restraints. Make sure the fittings are secure and the belts are functioning correctly.

## Travel checklist

As part of your planning, make a checklist of equipment, documents and other items.

If you're travelling through several countries, check against each item whether it's compulsory or strongly recommended.

### Emergency equipment

In many countries emergency equipment must be carried. Check with motoring organisations to find out what is required in the countries you will be visiting. This equipment may include



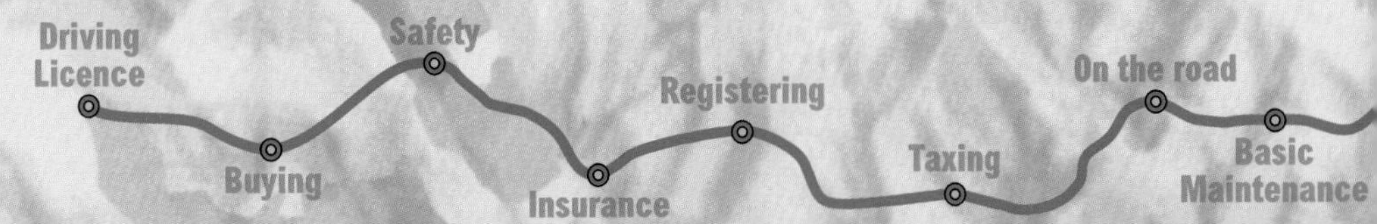

- emergency repair kits
- spare bulbs
- emergency windscreen
- emergency warning triangle
- fire extinguisher
- first aid kit
- snow chains.

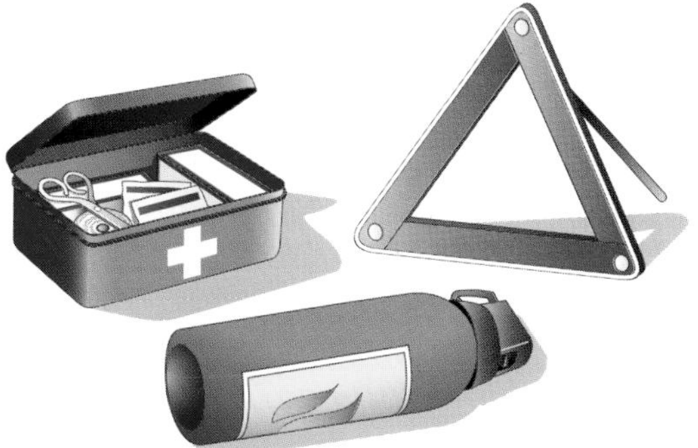

In some countries, if you carry skis or anything else on your roof, you may be required to do so in a purpose made box securely fitted to your roof rack. Bear in mind if you are travelling in extreme cold weather conditions you should be prepared for heavy snow. You should ensure you have blankets, food, drink and a shovel in your car.

## Documents

You must carry your national driving licence when motoring abroad. Even if you need an International Driving Permit (see page 186), take your national licence too. If you

want to drive a hired or borrowed vehicle in the country you're visiting, ask about minimum age requirements in case they apply to you.

In Italy, you must carry a translation with your licence. You can get this free of charge from the major motoring organisations. If you have a pink or pink and green EC-type UK licence, this translation isn't required.

Many non-EC countries still require an International Driving Permit (IDP). To qualify for one, you must be 18 or over.

To apply you'll need

- your driving licence
- a passport-sized photograph
- a fee.

The motoring organisations can issue your IDP.

Local Offices

You must also carry the original Vehicle Registration Document with you. If you don't have this, apply to a DVLA Local Office for a temporary certificate of registration (V379). Apply through your local Post Office well in advance of your journey.

If you plan to hire, borrow or lease a vehicle, you must ensure you have all the relevant documents.

If you have a disability and hold a Blue Badge you should



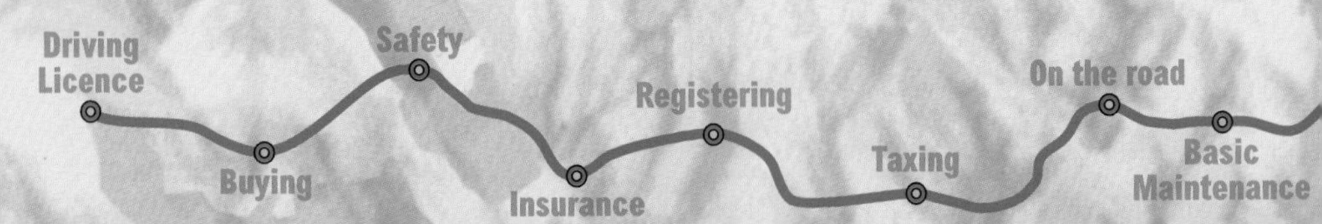

take it with you. Many European countries recognise and allow special parking for any vehicle displaying these badges.

## Motoring regulations

Don't drink and drive. The laws and penalties abroad are often more severe than those in the UK. You should check the following:

- fire extinguisher:
  - this is compulsory in some countries. In the event of a fire, get everyone clear of the car and ensure the emergency services are called
  - tackling a fire yourself can be dangerous
- advance warning triangle:
  - the use of a warning triangle is compulsory in most countries for all vehicles with more than two wheels. Hazard warning lights should not be used instead of a triangle, but to complement it. Some countries require two advance warning triangles
- spare bulbs:
  - some countries require you to carry a spare set of bulbs
- first aid kit:
  - make sure your vehicle carries a first aid kit. It is compulsory in some countries and strongly recommended in many others
- identification plate:
  - if you're towing a caravan or trailer, fit an identification plate

take it with you. Many European countries recognise and allow special parking for any vehicle displaying these badges.

## Motoring regulations

Don't drink and drive. The laws and penalties abroad are often more severe than those in the UK. You should check the following:

---

- fire extinguisher:
  - this is compulsory in some countries. In the event of a fire, get everyone clear of the car and ensure the emergency services are called
  - tackling a fire yourself can be dangerous
- advance warning triangle:
  - the use of a warning triangle is compulsory in most countries for all vehicles with more than two wheels. Hazard warning lights should not be used instead of a triangle, but to complement it. Some countries require two advance warning triangles
- spare bulbs:
  - some countries require you to carry a spare set of bulbs
- first aid kit:
  - make sure your vehicle carries a first aid kit. It is compulsory in some countries and strongly recommended in many others
- identification plate:
  - if you're towing a caravan or trailer, fit an identification plate

- nationality plate:
  - you must display a nationality plate of the approved size and design at the rear of your vehicle or caravan/trailer
- passengers:
  - never take more passengers than your vehicle is built to carry. Make sure you use your seat belts and everyone is secure before setting out on any journey
- speed limits:
  - there are speed limits in all countries, but they vary from country to country. A list of the speed limits can be obtained from the motoring organisations. Make sure you know the limits for those countries you will be travelling through. Obey all speed limits. Many countries have severe on-the-spot fines for offenders. Others prosecute, and that could prove to be expensive.

On-the-spot fines can be imposed for most minor motoring offences. Make sure you know the regulations for each country you intend visiting and obey them.

exports

## Going abroad for more than twelve months

- vehicles being taken out of Great Britain for more than 12 months must be notified as permanently exported
- the Registration Document will have to be surrendered before you go
- you will need a DVLA export certificate to enable you to re-register the vehicle in another country
- the vehicle will have to be re-registered abroad
- Japanese authorities require a special certificate showing date of manufacture or first registration.



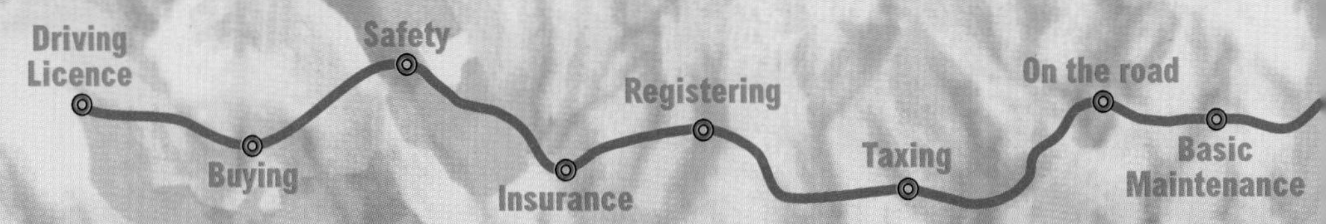

Vehicles used or kept in GB are registered at DVLA. The Channel Isles, Isle of Man and Northern Ireland have separate vehicle licensing authorities. If you intend to take the vehicle out of the country for more than 12 months, you must tell DVLA. Return the Registration Document to DVLA showing the date of export. In its place you will receive a certificate of export. This will facilitate re-registration abroad.

If you do not have the Registration Document, you will need to apply for an export certificate using form V756. Make sure the form contains all required information including the vehicle registration mark and the vehicle identification number (VIN).

Local Offices

Export certificates can be obtained over the counter at one of DVLA's 40 Local Offices (see chapter 15) provided you are the registered keeper. You can also apply on form V765, but proof of identity showing your name and address will be required. For example, a driving licence or utility bill could be used. The DVLA Local Office will not accept an application more than 14 days in advance.

## Frequently asked questions

### What if I break down?

Dealing with breakdowns abroad can be especially time consuming and worrying without the help of one of the

motoring organisations or breakdown services. If you belong to a breakdown service you can have it extended for going abroad. This will cost extra, but will be worth it for peace of mind.

The best prevention is to have your car thoroughly serviced before you leave and to make regular checks *en route*.

You can also make sure you're prepared for minor breakdowns.

### Do I need to let my insurance company know I am going?

Yes you do need to consult your insurer. Third party motor vehicle insurance is compulsory in most countries. It is strongly recommended you contact your insurer to make sure you're adequately covered. Most insurance policies issued in the UK automatically provide third party cover in EC countries as well as in some others. They do not provide comprehensive cover unless you arrange this with your insurer, who may charge an extra premium. Make sure you have the appropriate insurance certificate with you. Certain countries require a bail bond as a security in the event of an accident. Your insurer will be able to help you out with all these queries.



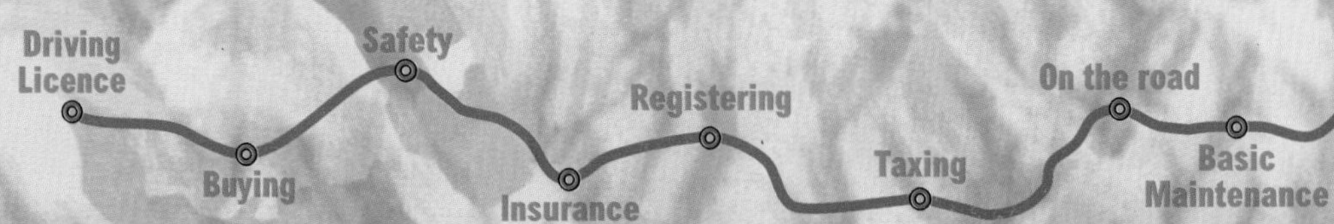

## Now we are in the European Union do I need a passport?

passports

Yes, all persons travelling must either hold, or be named on, an up-to-date passport valid for all countries through which you intend to travel. Carry your passport(s) at all times. Keep a separate note of the number, date and place of issue of each passport, in case they are stolen or lost.

Travellers need a visa for some European countries. Check well in advance with the embassies or consulates concerned. This is particularly important if you hold a UK passport not issued in this country, or the passport of any other country.

## What if one of us becomes ill while we are away?

You're strongly advised to take out comprehensive medical insurance cover for any trip abroad. Most medical treatment can be obtained free of charge or at reduced cost from the healthcare schemes of countries with whom the UK has reciprocal healthcare arrangements. However, don't rely on these arrangements alone.

The Department of Health leaflet E111 is available from any Post Office. It provides health advice for travellers.

**I haven't driven abroad before and we are booked to go this year. I am a bit nervous about driving on the right.**

It can take you time to adjust to driving on the right, and mistakes can lead to accidents. Get into the habit of using all your mirrors before making any manoeuvre, particularly before deciding to overtake. Remember to check the left exterior mirror where fitted.

Make certain you feel fit enough for your trip. Don't let your attention wander: it can be dangerous to forget where you are, even for a moment.

Each time you set out, remember that you're in a foreign country where you must drive on the right. Avoid driving for long periods and don't allow fatigue to set in. Take special care after a rest when you drive out onto the road again.

Hire vehicles will normally be left-hand drive. These may feel unfamiliar at first – make sure you understand the controls before you drive.

---

- take extra care at roundabouts. Be aware of the changed priority
- don't attempt to overtake until you're used to driving on the right
- take extra care at junctions.

---

Don't forget to adjust to driving on the left again as soon as you return!



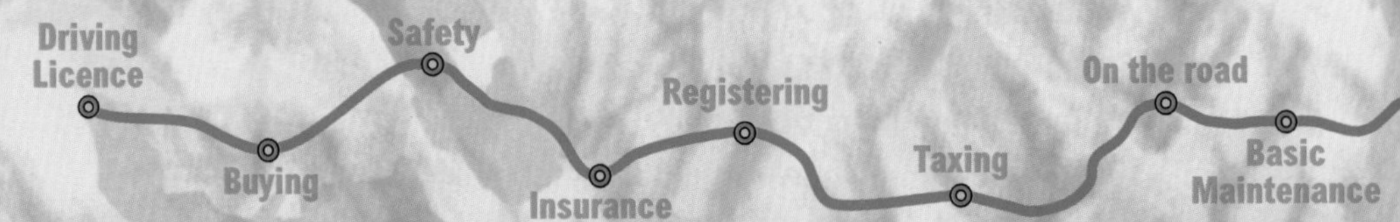

## Do you have to pay to drive on the motorways?

Some countries charge motorway tolls. You can find information about these from the motoring organisations and you should include the cost in your budget.

export

## Do I have to tell DVLA if I am taking my vehicle abroad for a long period?

If you are taking the vehicle abroad for more than 12 months you must notify DVLA of permanent export.

## Must I surrender the registration document?

Yes. In its place you will receive an export certificate to enable you to re-register abroad.

## What else will I need to re-register?

This depends on the country to which you are going. Some countries require further documentation, e.g. Japan (see below). All countries require sight of the GB export certificate. If the vehicle is already registered, apply to DVLA, Export Section, SA99 1BL [Tel 01792 783100].

## I am visiting Japan. Do I need a Special Certificate?

Yes, you will need to produce a special certificate showing date of first registration or date of manufacture. If the vehicle is new and unregistered, apply to the Vehicle Certification Agency. 1 Eastgate Office Centre, Eastgate Road, Bristol, BS5 6XX (Tel: 0117 951 5151).



## What if I need to relicense my vehicle while I am abroad?

If you need to relicense your vehicle before you return to Great Britain, you should apply by post on form V10 (you can get one at a main Post Office or any DVLA Local Office before you leave with an accompanying letter of explanation). It should be sent to a head Post Office in Great Britain about six weeks before the licence should start. Please give an address where the licence should be sent (an address abroad will do if you prefer) – but you must enter your British address on the V10. Please note that a foreign MOT certificate is not acceptable for a British vehicle licence application.



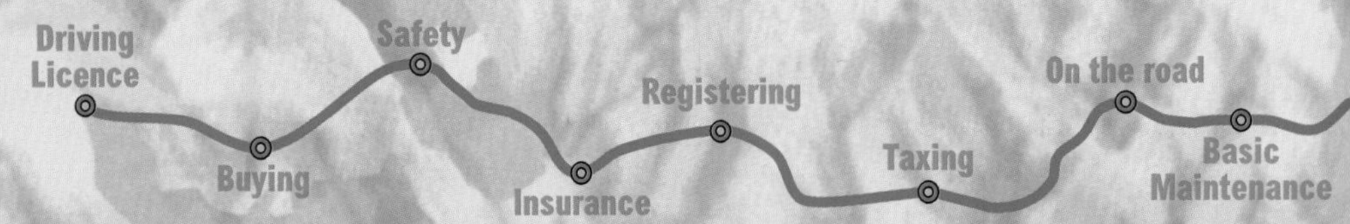

UK

Health
advice for
Travellers
anywhere in
the world
Vital Information on
Avoiding Health Risks
Planning for Healthy Travelling
Obtaining Emergency Medical Treatment
Form E111 – the passport to free or reduced-cost emergency medical treatment in most European countries



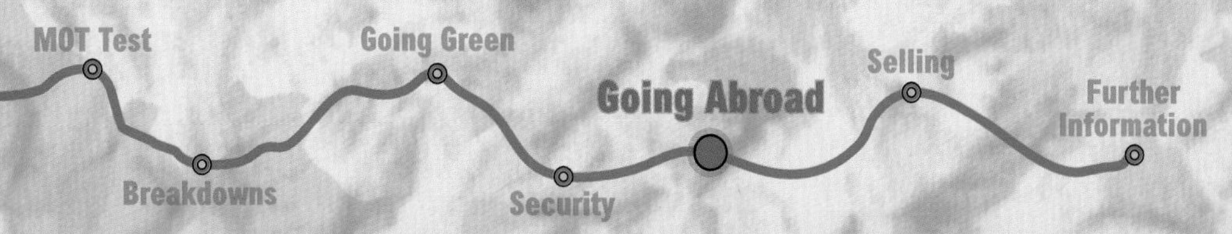
MOT Test
Going Green
Selling
Going Abroad
Further Information
Breakdowns
Security

chapter fourteen

# selling your car

preparation

selling privately

scrapping your vehicle

frequently asked questions

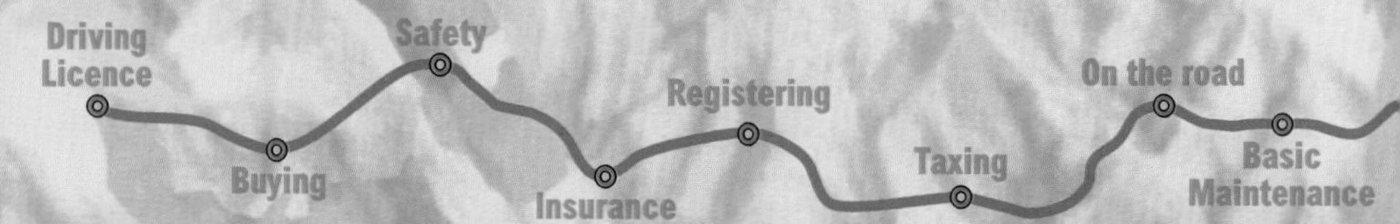

## Preparation

First impressions mean a lot, so you should ensure your car is spotless both inside and out before you advertise it. Get rid of any junk or litter, empty the ash trays and spray with air freshener. Ensure that it is topped up with oil and water. Check all the tyres too.

When preparing to sell your car, put yourself in the buyer's shoes. Ask yourself how much you would be prepared to pay for the car. You can use magazines and price guides to fix a fair price. Be honest with yourself; you could waste time and advertising money if you pitch the price too high. Be aware that the customer, whether a dealer or private buyer, may not be prepared to pay the asking price and make an offer instead. You may want to add a margin for haggling.

## Selling privately

Having ensured that your vehicle looks as though it is straight out of the showroom you should check that you have all the correct paperwork.



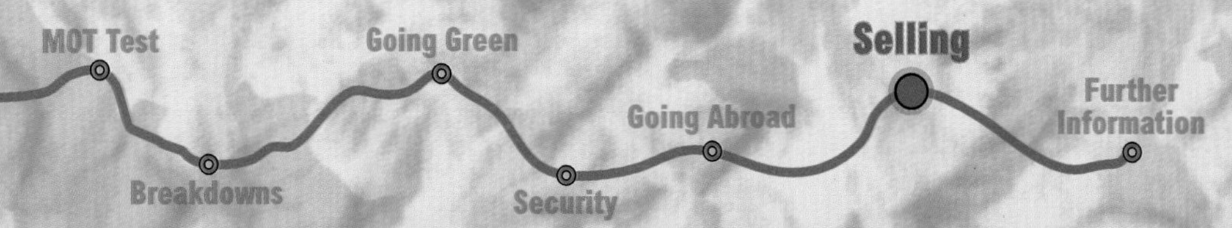

Make sure you have

- the Vehicle Registration Document
- a current MOT certificate (if three years old or over). If there is only a short time to run on this then it is advisable to have the vehicle tested. Although this does not guarantee the vehicle's roadworthiness at the time of selling, it could clinch the sale or add value
- any vehicle history:
  - service manual
  - garage bills
  - previous MOT certificates.

## Advertising

There are several ways you can do this

- word of mouth
- local shop windows
- via the Internet
- specialist car magazines
- local or national newspapers.

Keep the advert concise and honest.

When a potential buyer contacts you

- take their name and phone number
- make a precise appointment.

You may find it more comfortable to ensure you are not alone when the potential buyer calls. Be aware of your personal safety before you invite a stranger into your home.

## The paperwork

Registration Document

Failure to notify DVLA of a vehicle transfer is a criminal offence. As the seller you must

- send the Vehicle Registration Document back to DVLA if the document being used was issued after 1 March 1997
- make sure you receive payment before you part with the vehicle
- give the buyer a receipt and all relevant documentation relating to the vehicle
- fill in the vehicle's mileage details.

## Old style Registration Document

If you have a Registration Document issued before 1 March 1997, complete the tear-off slip, and return it at once to DVLA at the address shown on the form. Prompt notification will ensure that you are not blamed for any offences committed in the vehicle after it was transferred. Pass the top part of the form to the buyer and remind them to send it promptly to DVLA.

### New style Registration Document

For documents issued after 1 March 1997, you must complete the blue section. Both you and the buyer must sign and date the document. You have legal responsibility to send the form to DVLA. Give the green part to the buyer and destroy the red part.

If you are transferring the vehicle to a motor trader, the red part should be completed along with the vehicle's mileage information.

### Taking the money

Don't transfer the vehicle until you have received the total amount of money agreed for the sale.

If the buyer is paying cash, but does not have enough money with them, take a deposit. The remainder can be paid to you in cash, by cheque (wait for this to be cleared before parting with the car) or by a banker's draft. Check that neither of these are forgeries: telephoning the issuing bank or building society can confirm the issue.

## Scrapping your vehicle

If your vehicle is no longer roadworthy you may want to dispose of it rather than spend a large amount of money



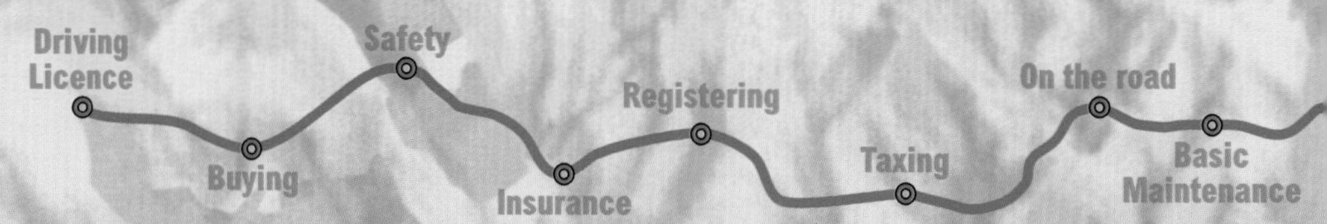

restoring it. You should do this responsibly by taking it to a scrap yard. Choose a scrap yard which is environmentally aware and is committed to recycling materials.

Alternatively some local authorities will accept or even collect the vehicle from you. You should seek advice from them on this.

Do not just abandon the vehicle as it can be traced back to you. If the vehicle is unlicensed and on the public road, enforcement action will still be taken against you for road tax evasion.

## The paperwork

You should only tell DVLA that a vehicle has been scrapped if you have actually broken it up, or destroyed it yourself.

If you want to keep its registration number you must transfer or retain it before disposal of the vehicle, otherwise entitlement to the number will be lost. For more



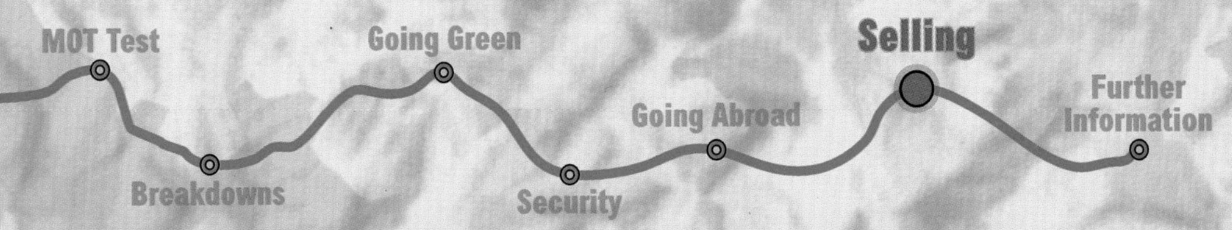

information, see booklet INF 46, available from DVLA Customer Enquiries Unit and DVLA Local Offices.

## Old style Registration Document

Please record scrapping on the back of the Registration Document.

If you dispose of the vehicle to an insurance company* in return for a total loss payment then you should tell DVLA that you have passed on the vehicle to the insurance company, using the 'Notification of Sale or Transfer' part of the Registration Document. Give the top part of the Document to the insurance company.

If you have sold or passed the vehicle on to someone else for scrap (including to a scrap dealer) simply tell DVLA of the transfer using the tear-off part of the Registration Document. Make sure you notify DVLA as soon as the vehicle changes hands. Hand the top part of the Document to the new keeper of the vehicle so that they can tell DVLA when they have scrapped it.

## New style Registration Document

Please record scrapping using the V5 blue top section.

If you dispose of a vehicle to an insurance company* in return for a total loss payment then you should



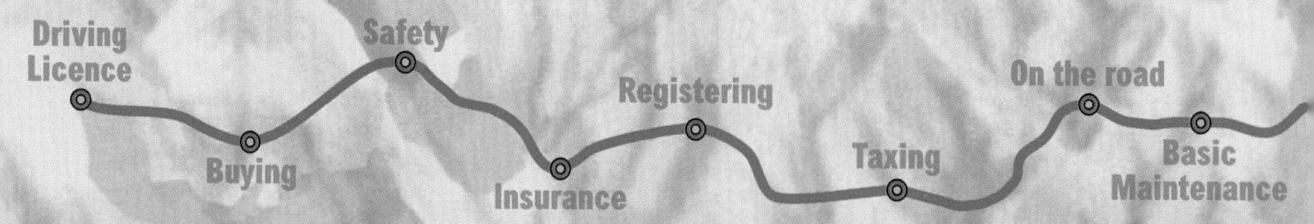

- give the V5 blue section together with the V5/2 green section to the insurance company*
- tell DVLA that you have passed on the vehicle to the insurance company*, using the V5/3 red section.

If you have sold or passed the vehicle on to someone else for scrap (including a scrap dealer) you should

- tell DVLA of the transfer using the V5/3 red section of the Registration Document
- give the V5 blue section together with the V5/2 green section to the new keeper of the vehicle so that the new keeper can tell DVLA when he or she has scrapped it.

*Please note: under a special arrangement between DVLA and the insurance industry, your insurer may ask you for the whole Registration Document (V5, V5/2, V5/3), which they will complete on your behalf and forward to DVLA. You may, if you prefer, follow the procedures given above and notify DVLA using the V5/3, or notify them of disposal by letter giving date of sale and name and address details.

## Frequently asked questions

### What could happen if I failed to tell DVLA of a transfer?

You would be guilty of a criminal offence and could be fined up to £1000. You may also be visited by the police or the



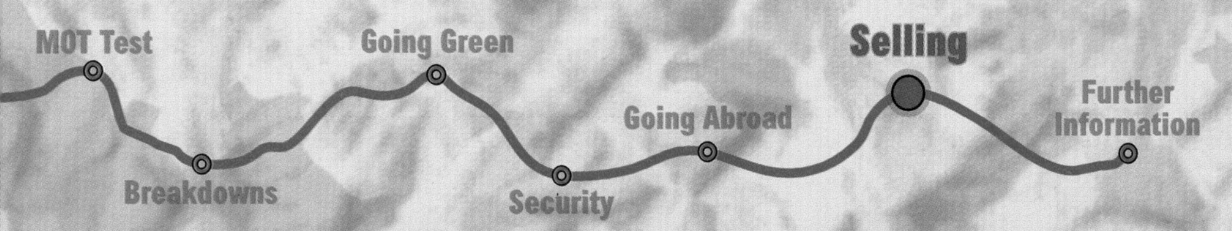

local authority if the vehicle is involved in a criminal offence or parking violation.

consumer advice

## How can I protect myself from fraud?

- ensure that you are paid in cash and never hand over the vehicle or the keys before you are paid in full
- if the buyer is paying by cheque or banker's draft, ring the issuing bank to check its authenticity
- ask the buyer for some form of identification.

## What should I give the buyer?

- a receipt which is signed, dated and which includes your personal details



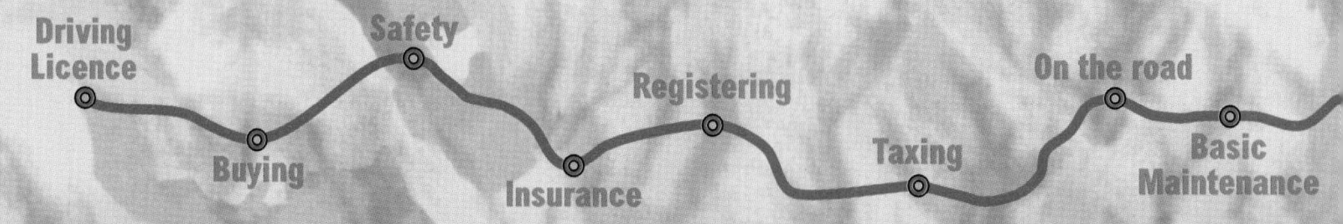

- all documentation including the relevant part of the registration document
- the current MOT certificate (and any old ones you may have kept)
- any vehicle history such as repair bills and service manual.

---

## Can I retain my personal number plate?

transfers

Yes, you can transfer it to another vehicle or retain it on a certificate for 12 months. There is a certain amount of paperwork to be done, check out the details in chapter 5 or the website.



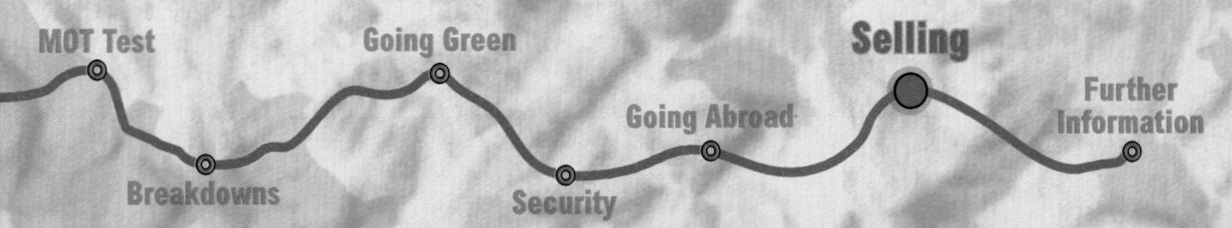

chapter fifteen

# further information

DVLA Local Offices

DVO Agencies

Post Offices

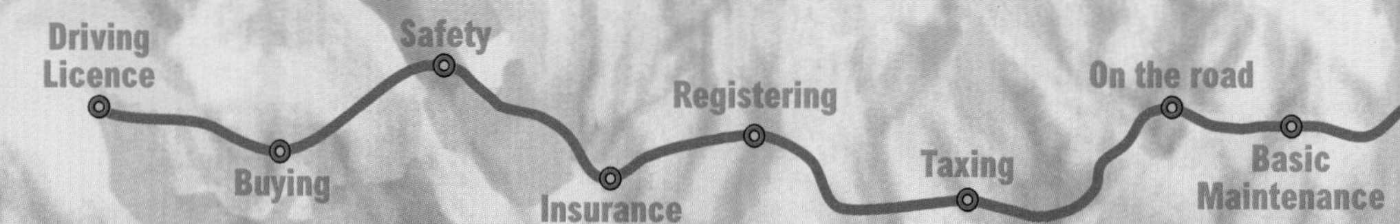

## DVLA Local Offices

Normally open 9.30 am – 4 pm Monday – Thursday, 9.30 am – 3.30 pm Friday. Some offices close for lunch. Also because of staff training, offices will not open until 10.30 am on the third Wednesday of every month.



### Scotland and North Area

| | |
|---|---|
| Aberdeen | Greyfriars House, Gallowgate,<br>Aberdeen AB10 1WG<br>Tel: 01224 648216 |
| Carlisle | Ground Floor, 3 Merchants Drive,<br>Parkhouse, Carlisle CA3 OJW.<br>Tel: 01228 539401/539402 |
| Dundee | Caledonian House, Greenmarket, Dundee<br>DD1 1DP<br>Tel: 01382 225765 |
| Edinburgh | Saughton House, Broomhouse Drive<br>Edinburgh EH11 3XE<br>Tel: 0131 455 7919 |
| Glasgow | 107 Bothwell Street, Glasgow G2 7EE<br>Tel: 0141 226 4161 |



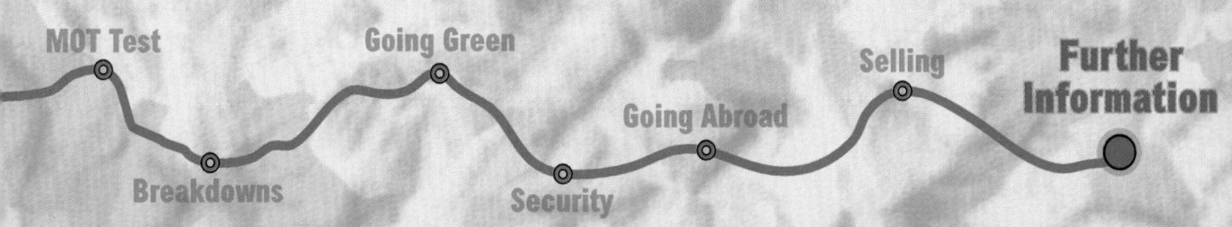

| | |
|---|---|
| Inverness | Longman House, 28 Longman Road<br>Inverness IV1 1SF<br>Tel: 01463 239321/239322 |
| Middlesbrough | 9th Floor, Corporation House,<br>73-75 Albert Road, Middlesbrough TS1 2BP<br>Tel: 01642 217722 |
| Newcastle | Eagle Star House, Regent Farm Road,<br>Newcastle Upon Tyne NE3 3QF<br>Tel: 0191 284 1026 |

## North and North Wales area

| | |
|---|---|
| Bangor | Penrhos Road, Penrhosgarnedd, Bangor<br>LL57 2JF<br>Tel: 01248 351822 |
| Birmingham | 2nd Floor, Edward House, Edward Street,<br>Birmingham B1 2RF<br>Tel: 0121 212 0155 |
| Chester | Norroy House, Nuns Road, Chester CH1 2ND<br>Tel: 01244 348195 |
| Leeds | 24a, Union Street, Leeds LS2 7JR<br>Tel: 01132 443035 |

| | |
|---|---|
| Manchester | Trafford House, Chester Road, Manchester<br>M32 0SL<br>Tel: 0161 872 8691 |
| Preston | Buckingham House, Glovers Court, Preston<br>PR1 4DQ<br>Tel: 01772 823911 |
| Shrewsbury | Whitehall, Monkmoor Road, Shrewsbury<br>SY2 5DR<br>Tel: 01743 366422/ 350511 |

### Eastern Area

| | |
|---|---|
| Beverley | Crosskill House, Mill Lane, Beverley<br>HU17 9JB<br>Tel: 01482 887884 |
| Ipswich | Podium Level, St. Clare House, Greyfriars<br>Ipswich IP1 1UT<br>Tel: 01473 258451 |
| Lincoln | Mill House, Brayford Side North, Lincoln<br>LN1 1YW<br>Tel: 01522 543681 |
| Luton | 2 Dunstable Road, Luton LU1 1EB<br>Tel: 01582 412143 |

| | |
|---|---|
| Northampton | Wootton Hall Park, Northampton NN4 0GA<br>Tel: 01604 762131 |
| Norwich | Rouen House, Rouen Road, Norwich<br>NR1 1UP<br>Tel: 01603 616411 |
| Nottingham | Block 6, Government Buildings, Chalfont Drive, Nottingham NG8 3RA<br>Tel: 0115 929 9924 |
| Peterborough | 88 Lincoln Road, Peterborough PE1 2ST<br>Tel: 01733 551671 |
| Sheffield | Bank House, 100 Queen Street, Sheffield<br>S1 1JX<br>Tel: 01142 722236 |

## South Wales and South Area

| | |
|---|---|
| Bournemouth | Tregonwell Court, 118 Commercial Road, Bournemouth. BH2 5LN<br>Tel: 01202 558531 |
| Bristol | Northleigh House, Lime Kiln Close, Stoke Gifford, Bristol BS34 8SR<br>Tel: 0117 969 2211 |

| | |
|---|---|
| Cardiff | Archway House, 77 Ty Glas Avenue,<br>Llanishen, Cardiff. CF4 5DX<br>Tel: 029 2075 3355 |
| Exeter | Hanover House, Manaton Close, Matford<br>Business Park, Exeter EX2 8EF<br>Tel: 01392 824330 |
| Oxford | Ground Floor, 3 Cambridge Terrace, Oxford<br>OX1 1RW<br>Tel: 01865 724056 |
| Portsmouth | 1-4 Queen Street, Portsmouth PO1 3JD<br>Tel: 023 8292 3627 |
| Reading | 77-81 Basingstoke Road, Reading RG2 0ER<br>Tel: 0118 987 1166 |
| Swansea | DVLC, Longview Road, Swansea SA99 1DE<br>Tel: 01792 783900 |
| Truro | Pydar House, Pydar Street, Truro TR1 2TG<br>Tel: 01872 278635 |
| Worcester | Clerkenleap Barn, Broomhall, Worcester<br>WR5 3HR<br>Tel: 01905 821720 |



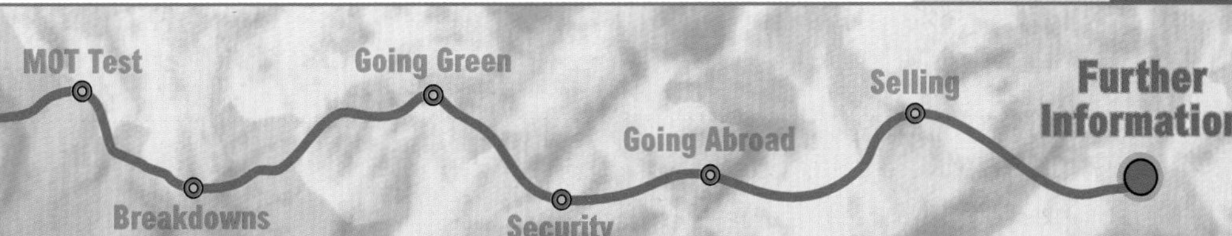

## South East Area

| | |
|---|---|
| Brighton | PO Box 357, Circus House, New England Road, Brighton BN1 1DH<br>Tel: 01273 692271 |
| Chelmsford | 2nd Floor, Parkway House, 49 Baddow Road, Chelmsford CM2 0XJ<br>Tel: 01245 281111 |
| Maidstone | Coronet House, 11 Queen Anne Road, Maidstone ME14 1XB<br>Tel: 01622 675432 |
| Sidcup | 12-18 Station Road, Sidcup, London DA15 7DA<br>Tel: 020 8302 2134 |
| Stanmore | Government Building, Canon Park, Honeypot Lane, Stanmore, Middlesex HA7 1BD<br>Tel: 020 8905 7400 |
| Wimbledon | Ground Floor Connect House, 133-137 Alexandra Road, Wimbledon SW19 7JY<br>Tel: 0870 600 6767 |



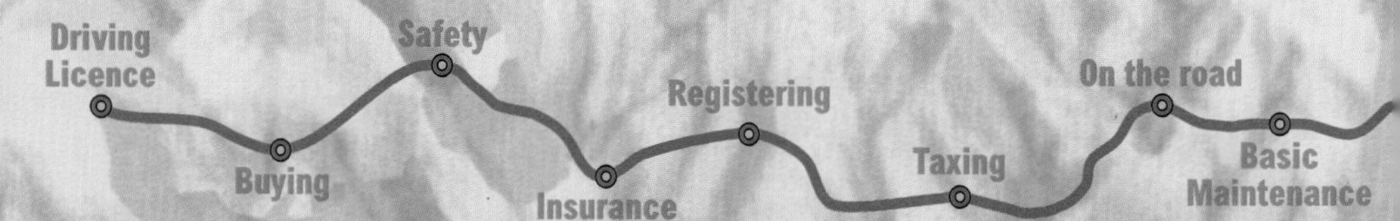

## DVO Agencies

### Driving Standards Agency – Test Enquiries and Booking Centre

DSA

DSA, PO Box 280, Newcastle upon Tyne NE99 1FP
Tel: 0870 01 01 372
Welsh speakers: 0870 01 00 372
Minicom: 0870 01 07 372
Fax: 0870 01 02 372

### Driving Standards Agency – Head Office

Stanley House, 56 Talbot Street, Nottingham NG1 5GU
Tel: 0115 901 2500
Fax: 0115 901 2940

### Vehicle Inspectorate

VI

Operations Centre, 91-92 The Strand, Swansea SA1 2DH
Tel: 01792 458888

Local Offices (VI)

For all MOT enquiries use MOT Enquiry Line 0845 600 5977 (local rate)



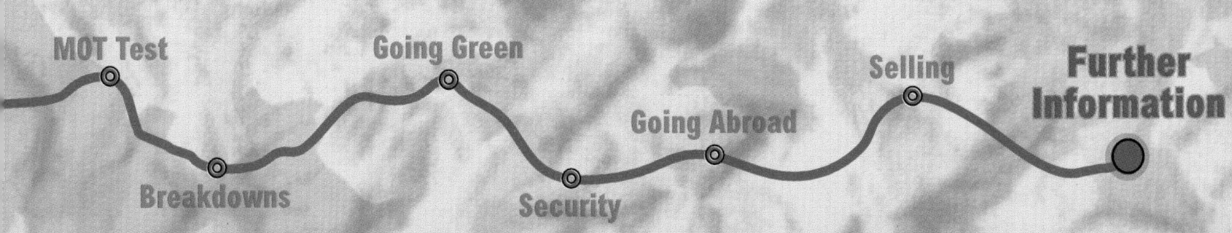

VI

**Vehicle Inspectorate - Head Office**

Berkley House, Croydon Street, Bristol BS5 0DA
Tel: 0117 954 3200

DVLA

**Driver and Vehicle Licencing Agency (DVLA)**

Customer Enquiry Unit, Swansea, SA6 7JL
Driver enquiries - tel: 0870 240 0009

Vehicle enquiries - tel: 0870 240 0010

VCA

**Vehicle Certification Agency**

1 Eastgate Office Centre, Eastgate Road, Bristol BS5 6XX
Tel: 0117 952 4191

HA

**Highways Agency Contacts**

TCFL

**Transport Committee for London**

TCSU

**Traffic Control Systems Unit**

## Post Offices

(for postal applications)

### England

Aldershot GU11 1AP
Altrincham WA14 1AA
Ashford TN23 1AA
Aylesbury HP20 1AB
Basildon SS14 1AA
Basingstoke RG21 1AB
Bath BA1 1AA
Bedford MK40 1AB
Birmingham B18 6JS
Blackburn BB1 6AT
Blackpool FY1 1AA
Bletchley MK2 2AA
Bolton BL1 1AD
Boston PE21 6AA
Bournemouth BH1 1XX
Bradford BD1 3HN
Brighton BN1 1BA
Bristol BS1 3XX
Bromley BR1 1AA
Burnley BB11 1DY
Bury St Edmunds IP33 1AA
Cambridge CB2 3AA
Canterbury CT1 2BA
Carlisle CA1 1AA
Chelmsford CM1 1XS
Colchester CO1 1AA
Coventry CV1 1AD
Crawley RH10 1AA
Crewe CW1 2HP
Darlington DL1 1AB
Derby DE1 1AA
Doncaster DN1 1AA
Dorchester DT1 1DH
Dudley DY1 1PW
Durham DH1 3RE
Exeter EX1 1AH
Gatwick RH6 0NU
Glenrothes KY7 5LN
Gloucester GL1 1AD
Grantham NG31 6AA
Great Yarmouth NR30 1AB
Grimsby DN31 1UU
Harlow CM20 1AA
Harrogate HG1 1AA
Harrow HA1 1AA
Haslemere GU27 2AF
Hastings TN34 1AA
Hemel Hempstead HP1 1DQ
High Wycombe HP13 5ES
Huddersfield HD1 1AA



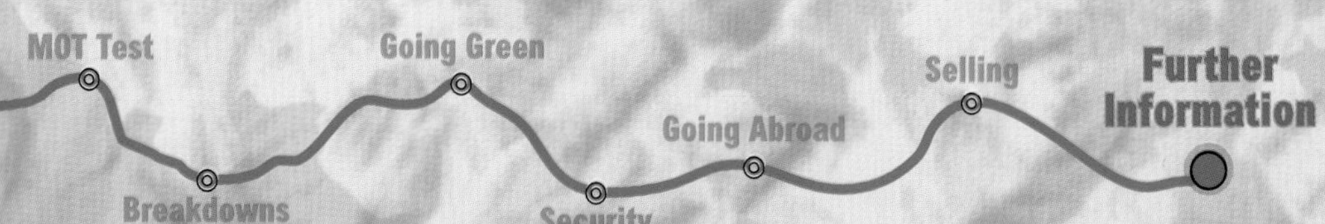

Hull HU9 1EA

Ilford IG1 1AA

Ipswich IP4 1ER

Kings Lynn PE30 1YB

Lancaster LA1 1AA

Leeds LS1 2UH

Leicester LE1 6AJ

Lincoln LN1 1AA

Liverpool L1 1AA

London *(see separate list)*

Luton LU1 2LP

Maidstone ME14 1BP

Manchester M2 1BB

Morpeth NE61 1AA

Newcastle-U-Tyne NE1 7AB

Newport (IOW) PO30 1AA

Northampton NN1 1AF

Norwich NR1 3DD

Nottingham NG1 2BN

Oldham OL1 3HB

Oxford OX1 1ZZ

Peterborough PE1 1AB

Plymouth PL1 1AB

Portsmouth P01 1AA

Preston PR1 1AB

Reading RG1 2DG

Salisbury SP1 1AB

Scarborough YO11 1AA

Sheffield S1 1AB

Slough SL1 1DU

Southampton S014 2PH

Southend-on-Sea SS1 1LL

Stevenage SG1 1QR

Stockport SK1 1QF

Stoke-on-Trent ST1 1AA

Sunderland SR1 3LL

Swindon SN1 1QW

Taunton TA1 1AB

Torquay TQ1 1AD

Truro TR1 2AP

Tunbridge Wells TN1 2AD

Wakefield WF1 3BD

Walsall WS1 1AA

Warrington WA1 1QB

Wigan WN1 1AA

Wolverhampton

Worcester WR1 1AA

York YO1 2DA

## Scotland

Aberdeen AB9 1GG

Bathgate EH48 4AA

Dumfries DG1 1AA

Dundee DD1 1AA

Dunfermline KY12 7AA

Edinburgh EH1 3SR
Falkirk FK1 1AA
Fort William PH33 6AA
Galashiels TD1 1AA
Glasgow G2 5QX
Inverness IV1 1AA
Kirkwall KW15 1AA
Lerwick ZE1 0AA
Motherwell ML1 1BA
Perth PH2 8AF
Stirling FK8 2BP
Stornoway HS1 2AD
Wick KW1 4BS

## Wales

Bangor LL57 1AA
Caerphilly CF8 IUD
Haverfordwest SA61 1AA
Llanelli SA15 1AA
Newport (Gwent) NP9 1AZ
Pontypridd CF37 2SN
Swansea SA6 8AQ

## London Postal Districts

(EC1-4) (EC99) (E1-18) (RM1-18)– London East District Office, Ilford, IG1 1AA

(NW1-NW11) London West District Office, Harrow, HA1 1AA

(N1-N22) (W1-W14) (WC1-2) London, N1 1AB

(SE1-SE28) (BR1-BR8) (CR0) (CR2-4) (CR9) (DA1-DA18) (SM1-SM7) London South East District Office, Bromley BR1 1AA

(SW1- SW20) (TW1-TW20) (KT1-KT24) London South West District Office, SW5 9RB

## Index

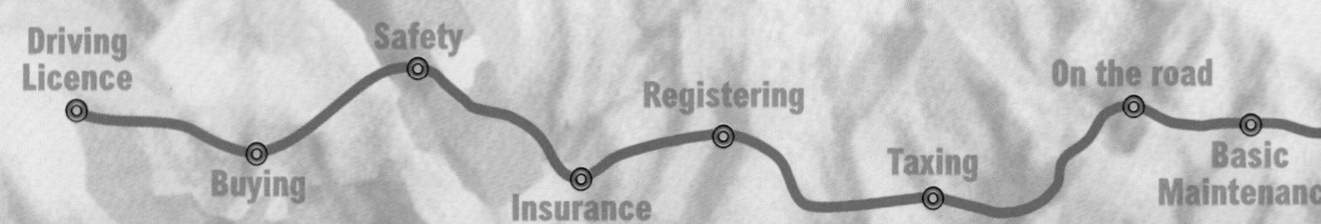

Driving Licence
Buying
Safety
Insurance
Registering
Taxing
On the road
Basic Maintenanc

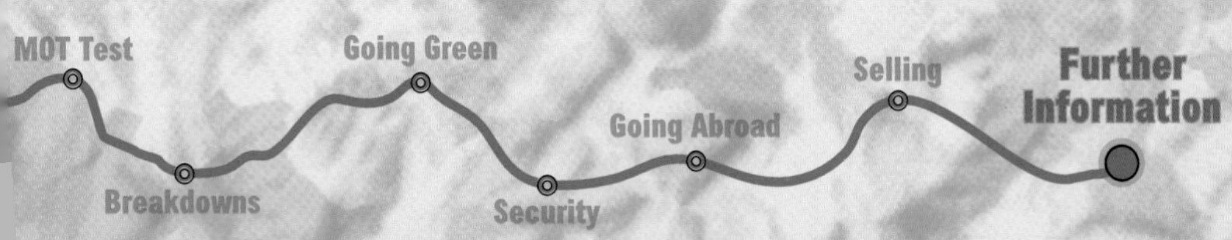
MOT Test
Going Green
Selling
Further Information
Going Abroad
Breakdowns
Security

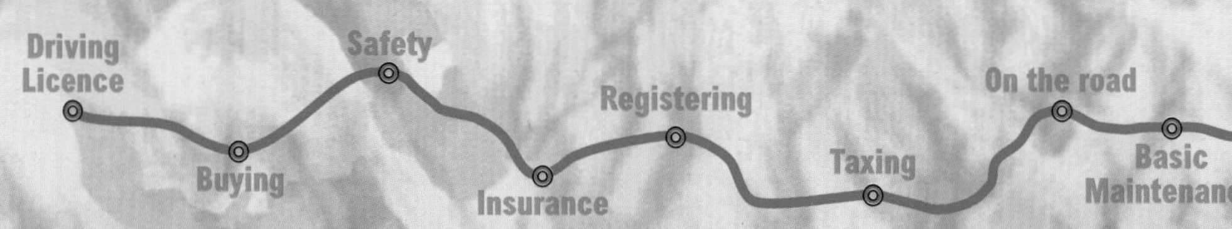
Driving Licence
Buying
Safety
Insurance
Registering
Taxing
On the road
Basic Maintenanc